# PATIO GARDENING

## ■ Step by Step to Growing Success ■

### ■ Yvonne Rees & David Palliser ■

CROWOOD GARDENING GUIDES

First published in 1991 by
The Crowood Press Ltd
Gipsy Lane
Swindon
Wiltshire SN2 6DQ

© The Crowood Press Ltd 1991

**British Library Cataloguing in Publication Data**

1. Patio gardening.

Rees, Yvonne
  Patio gardening.
  1. Patios and roof gardens. Plants. Cultivation
  I. Title II. Palliser, David
  635.9671

ISBN 1 85223 507 1

**Picture Credits**
Front cover photograph: B & Q Ltd (exhibitor), David Stevens (designer),
Steven Wooster (photographer).
Larch Lap for Figs 5, 64 and 66; B & Q Ltd for Fig 7; Unwins Seeds Ltd for Fig 15; Hozelock for Figs 16, 86, 88 and 90; Noral Lighting Ltd for Fig 18; Marshalls for Fig 19; Bradstone for Figs 52 and 81; Delux for Fig 54; Geoff and Faith Whiten for Fig 74; Hickmet for Fig 94; Frank Odell for Figs 107, 110 and 111; and Dave Pike for Figs 115, 116, 117, 118, 120, 121, 123, 124, 128, 129, 131 and 133. All other photographs by the authors.

Typeset by Avonset, Midsomer Norton, Bath
Printed and bound by Times Publishing Group, Singapore

# Contents

# Preface

At the outset, creating a patio may seem like one of the most daunting tasks you could tackle in the garden; there are foundations to dig, flooring to be laid, features to plan and the whole area to decorate and furnish, as carefully as any kitchen or sitting room. Yet the lure of owning one is so strong that the benefits can easily outweigh the possible effort and expense involved. The patio performs many functions: it enables you to enjoy the garden at the slightest hint of good weather; it relieves the pressure on indoor living areas; it can become an outdoor kitchen, dining room, lounge and even playroom or office. It is adaptable, capable of embracing any garden style, incorporates a great many practical features, yet looks smart and stylish within any size, shape and location from roof to basement. Above all, this is an area of the home that can be enjoyed by absolutely everyone, whether young, old or disabled, and which suits every lifestyle. Once installed, the well-planned patio is little trouble to maintain.

It sounds like paradise — and is easy to believe, when sitting back in a comfortable chair enjoying the sunshine, surrounded by beautiful plants and flowers. If, however, you can't wait to enjoy this idyll for yourself or major construction work is not practical or affordable, there is always the option of creating an instant patio. This can be done, using loose-laid sections of timber decking, freestanding screens and partitions, and plenty of plants in containers — to create a truly moveable feast that can even go with you, lock, stock, and 'strawberry' barrel when you move.

You will find ideas and directions for all kinds of patio styles and features in this book, as well as a look at the plants, pots, ornaments, furniture and accessories that add the comfort and create the style. Designing and furnishing a patio can be great fun, and we hope you will enjoy planning that mini paradise of your own beyond the back door as much as you will delight in using it over the many seasons to come.

*Fig 1 (Opposite) A vigorous climber will transform plain walls into a curtain of colour and interest.*

*Fig 2 These raised beds have an ornamental lattice-work edging.*

CHAPTER 1

# The Room Outdoors

The patio is a wonderful hybrid between house and garden; and as a kind of outdoor living area, it provides valuable extra living space as well as an overspill area for the home during finer weather. It is planned, furnished and decorated very like any interior, yet it is unmistakeably a part of the garden, enjoying the benefits of sunshine and fresh air, decorated with living plants and furnished with sturdy weather-resistant materials such as stone and timber. Its use is extended beyond the seasons, because it provides a firm, dry surface, shelter from draughts and sometimes also from showers. It is the ideal area to site dining and lounging furniture or a barbecue, in order to enjoy an outdoor living, dining or cooking area.

A patio can be any size and shape, and can be sited wherever is most convenient and enjoyable. Ideally, it should open directly off the house (or sometimes apartment) but although this is preferable, it is not essential. The advantage is not just that you can step straight on to the patio from your kitchen, dining room or sitting room without having to negotiate the main garden. But the proximity to the house makes it easier to fetch drinks, food, and any other item you fancy taking outdoors. There are aesthetic as well as practical benefits too. As an outdoor extension of the home, it helps to make that transition from indoors to out as visually smooth as possible. This will create the impression that the room immediately beyond continues further and is indeed larger than it really is. This impression can be encouraged by the use of large picture windows and patio doors which are predominantly glass and can be slid right back in fine weather, making the distinction between home and patio even less easy to identify, as well as making access easy. French windows are the traditional entry point on to a patio or terrace, and although these window-style doors do not always allow an uninterrupted view of the garden when closed, they usually do when open. For an older style property they have a far more traditional appearance. French windows can be single, double or even in multiples.

It is important to blend interior and exterior together by carefully planning your choice of style and materials. A patio can have a distinctive atmosphere in the same way as any room, and it makes sense to match it to that of the room immediately within, as this will encourage a sense of continuity and pleasure. Thus you may choose a rustic cottage theme — old-fashioned flowers mimicking the pretty chintzes and sprig-patterned wallpapers indoors. Alternatively, if your home has a modern minimalist or exotically oriental design, the patio can take on the same tone with a clever choice of materials and accessories. For either of these designs, you could use a few architectural plants with bold, unusual shapes like bamboo and hostas — both good subjects for tubs and containers — against a background of stone, metal and timber used in strong, geometric designs.

There are other ways of blurring the boundaries between home and garden. Large leafy plants like Benjamin fig or the Swiss Cheese Plant, *Monstera deliciosa*, will grow to the ceiling in containers indoors, flourishing in the good light from large patio doors or picture windows and providing the perfect visual link with greenery outside. Flooring can also make that link if chosen carefully; for example, a surface that is attractive enough to be used in the kitchen or sitting room, yet tough enough to withstand the weather outside. An identical or similar material carried right through will make both areas seem much larger and certainly lead the eye towards the garden from the room indoors. This might be ceramic floor tiles (providing they are recommended as frost resistant), brick or stone. Using timber can also be particularly effective: parquet, stripped and polished boards or wood block flooring indoors, and timber decking laid outdoors. This can be a useful way to resolve an awkward change of level too as the decking can be slightly raised or stepped as required. More unusually, a stretch of water may be used to make that visual link (*see* page 73). An outdoor pool butted up to a floor-to-ceiling plate-glass window with a corresponding pool indoors may take time and effort to construct and maintain, but looks stunning.

Apart from its obvious appeal as an outdoor

living area, the patio can play a wide variety of roles depending on its position, the way it is designed and the owner's lifestyle. In a cramped city backyard, a small paved area hemmed in by high walls may be all the garden there is, so it needs to be multi-functional, and well planned to fit in all the plants and features wanted. Alternatively, it may form part of a much larger garden plan and have a quite specific purpose. The patio may surround the swimming pool, in which case an attractive surface suitable for lounging furniture will be given priority over plants, which might pollute the water. You may wish to create a fully fitted barbecue area or a small paved space for seating in a sunny spot in the garden or in front of a summer house. The patio can also be a formal decorative area with ornamental paving, statuary and colour co-ordinated blooms or simply a firm, dry surface immediately outside the backdoor where the children can play under

Fig 3   *A cobbled courtyard suits a town or country house and creates an instantly mature effect immediately beyond the back door.*

*Fig 4 In a small town or city garden, it is often worth converting the whole site into a sophisticated patio complex, which is divided into separate areas for different features.*

supervision from the house. It can be used to enjoy alfresco meals or just to take full advantage of any fine weather. A secluded and well-sheltered patio may even serve as an outdoor health spa – fitted with a sunken hot water spa bath or hot tub where the bubbling, steaming warm water can be enjoyed by family and friends all year round.

Because the patio is often well sheltered, especially in small city gardens where surrounding buildings and probably high levels of pollution raise the temperature by several degrees – it can be a real suntrap, a facility to be exploited not just by creating sunbathing areas, but by seizing the opportunity to grow a selection of more tender plants. Another important facility of the patio is that it is generally easy to maintain. Surfaces are neatly paved, tiled or timbered; plants are contained in raised beds or tubs and pots; furniture, features and accessories are smartly organized, often fully built-in to the general scheme. If the area is well planned, normal garden chores can be reduced to the absolute mimimum: the watering of containers in summer (although mulching and automatic systems can

help reduce this chore); the replacement of seasonal plants when past their prime to maintain a good display; and a general clear-up at the end of the year. It is ideally suited to the modern day garden lover looking for an attractive place to escape to and unwind, but whose busy, stressful lifestyle leaves little time to actually work on the area.

It may look quaintly cottage style, ornately Victorian or classically Georgian, as often as it adopts a sleek, modern appearance. However, the term patio is a relatively new one. The neatly paved area immediately beyond the house and leading the eye towards beautifully landscaped gardens beyond was originally called the terrace – and still is, behind many traditional period homes. It tends to be narrower than most patio areas but in many respects is just the same, stretching across the width of the back of the house, smartly paved and providing the ideal place to position an elegant table and chairs, tubs of plants and sometimes statuary. A low ornamental wall with decorative balustrades and steps down usually links the terrace to the rest of the garden.

# CHAPTER 2

# The Master Plan

Hopefully, your patio is going to be used extensively, probably more than any other part of the garden. It will not only provide facilities in good weather and bad, but with outdoor lighting or even a few candles in jam jars, it can be enjoyed in the evenings too. A well-lit patio can be used for a pre-dinner drink among the fragrance of honeysuckle and night-scented stocks, or as the setting for a full-scale dinner party with friends. It is important then that the area is carefully chosen and thoughtfully planned to meet your particular needs, and that it operates efficiently as well as looks good. This requires time spent at the early stages considering position, size and, ultimately, style and materials. As well as your own particular preferences, budget will be an important consideration here. Costs must be calculated right the way through, as they will affect your choice of materials and the size of finished patio. If you can see where the money is going before you commit yourself, it makes it easier to amend your ideas by substituting a less expensive material here, or a different, less elaborate feature there, without making any real compromises on style or effect. This need not produce an inferior product: the old saying, 'necessity is the mother of invention', can work to your advantage because by being forced to examine your plans more closely and tighten them up, you will often produce better results.

## BEST POSITION FOR YOUR PATIO

Ideally a patio should be sited where it will receive maximum warmth and sunshine. Since this is a feature you will want to use as frequently as possible and hopefully you will be able to enjoy it through most of the seasons. It is traditionally a place to relax and perhaps grow more tender or exotic plants and where more expensive furniture and features can be positioned. While a south-facing suntrap can always be screened and shaded to make it more comfortable for lounging and dining, a chilly, damp, north-facing paved area can be very bleak and you just won't feel like rushing out to use it very often. This will be particularly true if there are warmer, sunnier spots in the garden, so your efforts in designing and installing the patio will be wasted. Sometimes, however, there simply is no other option: the site may be so small or limited that a poorly orientated area is the only place where your patio can be put. In this case, you have to plan more carefully to compensate; by making sure the area is well sheltered, using warm colours like red brick and bright flowers, maybe even semi-enclosing the area in a style resembling the classic veranda. This style is often sheltered overhead and to waist height, sometimes including glass or Perspex panels which offer shelter without obscuring views of the garden.

The most convenient position for a terrace or patio is immediately by the house. It not only makes a neat transition between home and garden, but is also a sort of hybrid area that includes elements of both indoors and out: its paved area functions not only as a visual connection between both but is also useful for preventing dirt and other debris being trodden into the house. The patio looks good too, from the window or patio doors when the weather is too cold or wet to venture outside, and is handy for

*Fig 5   Ornamental patio walling and a timber pergola overhead
determine the seating area within this large, well-planned patio.*

taking out furniture, food and other items you may need from the house on sunny days. Steps or a formal balustrade are also a useful idea for the patio as they are often designed to make the transition from the house to the garden a smooth one, because they lead the eye towards softer landscaping features such as a low wall or raised beds, and the main garden.

However, where the back of the building is rather inhospitable and you do have a choice of position, your main patio may be better sited at the opposite end of the garden in a sunny corner or to one side. In this case, it is a good idea to provide good, dry access from the house in the form of a brick, stone or gravel path or stepping

stones if there is a lawn to be crossed. This makes reaching the patio easier and more comfortable, especially when the ground is waterlogged after rain. A chalet or log cabin summer house – which can be as modest as a simple wooden shelter affair, or more elaborately incorporate several rooms, window-boxes and a pitched roof – is frequently positioned where it will face maximum sunshine, away from the house. If this is where you like to spend a lot of your time in fine weather, it makes sense to plan a patio at the front of your summerhouse, so that you can enjoy its benefits more fully. Often the summerhouse doors are designed to open right back on to such an area, enabling you to sit within its shelter, half in and half out or right in full sunshine, depending on the weather and your mood. A summerhouse is also useful for storing all your patio furniture and barbecue accessories when not in use.

In the larger garden – and it need not be that large – there is no reason why you should not have several patio areas, in different styles and serving different purposes. Thus, you might plan an area for sunbathing as well as a small, enclosed area designed to be at its best in autumn and winter, or simply a separate and easily maintained spot dedicated to herbs, roses or your favourite plants, all grown in pots and containers. Dividing the garden into small areas or 'rooms' like this, screening them well and linking them by paths, so that you can wander round and 'discover' them or use them as a retreat, is an excellent way to make the general plot more interesting and to add an element of surprise and mystery.

In the smaller garden, the patio serves a different purpose. Indeed, it may be a good idea in a cramped town or city backyard, to convert the whole area to a paved, easy-to-maintain area, with the plants in containers or raised beds. This way you solve the problem of poor, over-used soil, as plants in pots and beds are better able to withstand pollution; and seasonal planting easily maintains a year-round display of interest. For where space is limited, it is the patio which takes on a prime importance, especially for city dwellers with busy lifestyles. However small, an outdoor retreat can be a godsend, as it relieves pressure on the home if you can relax or eat meals outdoors in fine weather. And if well planned, the combination of fresh air, the scent and sight of living plants and the sound of birds and maybe running water, is an excellent antidote to stress. For both aesthetic and practical reasons, it makes sense not to break up a small area into a token patio which is probably too tiny for practical use, especially since conventional grass and flower beds will still require tedious maintenance. You will make the garden look larger and far more interesting if you design a multi-purpose patio complex to encompass the total area and which, depending on available space, might include all the features you want. This patio complex could incorporate a variety of features including special areas for plants, seating,

Fig 6   The patio need not be sited next to the house: clever planning and design can create a multi-functional area anywhere in the garden that enjoys plenty of sunshine.

*Fig 7   A smart patio and comfortable furniture are the making of a lovely outdoor pool.*

playing, pools and fountains, changes of level, arches, pergolas and small garden buildings such as summerhouses, gazebos and a greenhouse.

There may be other occasions where a patio is an attractive and desirable part of a much larger garden plan. It makes sense to have one around the swimming pool for example, as a clean, paved area is important, not just for sunbeds, tables and chairs, but also to prevent dirt, stones and leaves being trodden into the water. Paving materials chosen must be easy to sweep and suitable to withstand the chemical effect of chlorinated water. Planting beds or containers must be kept well away from the edge of the pool. The surrounding area can usually be well screened with fast-growing conifers, high screens or panel fencing for privacy and comfort.

A centrally placed patio can be an interesting and striking feature in the right setting. In the middle of a formal lawn, a paved area with some ornamental centre-piece such as a statue, bird-

bath, sundial or fountain, makes a fine focal point and a good contrast of style and texture. Here, the patio has a purely visual function and may be further decorated with formal tubs or containers of plants – giving a far different look from the massed effect of flowers in more conventional cut-out planting beds. Alternatively, the patio can be sunken, which is a clever treatment for an awkward natural dip or hollow. The sunken garden tends to feature a symmetrical pattern of paths and paved areas with planting beds and seating positioned around in order to enjoy the sense of privacy and peace such as a garden offers. Often, a limited planting theme will be chosen to emphasize its separateness and special status away from the main garden. A sunken rose garden is popular, as many types and varieties of rose can be used to give choice of shape and colour and a long season of consecutive blooms. A single or two-colour scheme is equally effective, especially if soft, relaxing shades are chosen such

Fig 8   A sunken patio area situated anywhere in the garden where there
is a natural dip or hollow, is an intriguing and practical way to deal with
what could be a difficult landscaping problem.

Fig 9   Even a small balcony can be transformed into the perfect place to
sit and enjoy the sunshine and grow a few plants in pots.

as white, cream or soft blues and mauves. You should be able to select plants with flowers or foliage of the correct shade to carry you right through the seasons. However, a predominance of strong, hot reds or dazzling yellows does not work as well in a confined space like this.

Sometimes, there is a strong case for a patio to be positioned at the front of the house. If it is the sunniest spot and can be adequately secluded, it can serve all the usual patio functions quite happily. Sometimes the rear garden is also too small or even non-existent. Ideally, it should be possible to screen the area from the normal access path to the front door to avoid any intrusion on privacy from callers. In town areas, plants, particularly those around the boundaries, may have to be tough to resist pollution, tall to screen the patio and dense to filter out fumes and rubbish.

There is also no reason why homes with no garden at all should not enjoy the facilities of a patio, albeit on a small scale. Flats and apartments often have small balconies which can be given the same treatment using some form of decking or paving to dress up the area underfoot and make a stable surface for a table and a couple of chairs. Plants in tubs and containers might include a vigorous climber to clothe the vertical screens that usually offer privacy and protection on either side. Bright spring bulbs and summer annuals will add colour, and trailing species that can be trained to cascade over the railings and down the wall will disguise any unflattering features. Even small shrubs or pot-grown vegetables such as peppers and tomatoes can be grown. The well-furnished balcony, although often limited in size, provides a delightful place to enjoy an alfresco pre-dinner drink or a leisurely Sunday breakfast. Alternatively, it can be filled with plants to provide a wonderful breath of fresh air and living greenery to the room within. There are practical points which must be considered when planning a balcony area. You must check that it is strong enough to take the weight of furniture, pots and plants, as some balconies are purely ornamental and are not structurally designed for any other purpose. Its elevated position makes the balcony rather exposed so screening in tough but lightweight trelliswork or Perspex is usually essential. And since the area is usually limited in size, it makes sense to measure any furniture and containers very carefully to make sure they will fit the space available.

City dwellers lacking a garden and desperate for an area outdoors that they can call their own, have been moving upwards and looking at the roof as a possible patio area. A patio design is certainly the most practical treatment since, as with balconies, the most important factors to be considered are the possible load-bearing weight and ease of maintenance. At this height, exposure can also be cruel, and some form of shelter for plants as well as humans is essential if they are to flourish. Even so, it is advisable to select tough, vigorous species for roof-top sites. If the site is very windy, you will find a non-solid screen more effective than a solid one which offers too much resistance and will either break under the strain or funnel the wind unpleasantly. To save on weight, you should select only the lightest paving materials; sections of timber decking are particularly good for this purpose and are quick and easy to lay over most surfaces. Plant containers can also be extremely heavy, especially when filled with damp soil. You should avoid weighty containers like terracotta and stone, choosing instead timber tubs or fibreglass pots which conveniently come in a great many sizes and styles imitating other materials. Soil composts also vary greatly in weight, the peat-based types being much heavier, so you should try and use the lighter types. If saving on weight makes pots unstable in strong winds, particularly where they have been planted with taller plants, you may have to consider anchoring the pots in some way. The same rules apply to patio furniture; lightweight plastic and aluminium styles may be saving you on the kilos, but they need to be stable, and they will need to be stored safely when not in use. These difficult conditions make the roof-top patio a tricky area to plan successfully, but, well screened and with the right plants, it can be a delightful escape with breath-

Fig 10   You can often make the most of limited space in towns and cities by converting a flat roof area into a delightfully secluded patio area.

taking views. You should not forget at the earliest planning stages, that some form of convenient access to the roof is vital if the patio is going to be well used. Maintenance will naturally be kept to the minimum, but you will still have to work out some way of getting water to your plants without trotting up and down with cans or buckets. A small pump may be necessary to supply an outside roof-mounted tap or hosepipe if water pressure is insufficient.

## SHAPES AND SIZES

The area available will often be the determining factor that decides the size of your patio. In the majority of cases, it stretches naturally across the full width of the house or summerhouse for neatness and convenience, then down towards the garden to create a hopefully not too narrow rectangle or a neat square. Where the property is detached or semi-detached, the paved area might be continued round it, providing access from various points of the building and a wider range of features. If your patio is to be sited elsewhere in the garden, you will be limited only by the proximity of other planned or immoveable features and by the size of area you are prepared – or can afford – to screen off and pave. It seems that no area is too small; the classic postage stamp-sized backyard or balcony, converted to a patio and thoughtfully furnished with the right paving and features, is still charming and a pleasure to use. Carefully designed, its size can be turned to advantage to create a cosy outdoor living area or stylish-looking area based on a particular theme to be enjoyed both from the house and garden. The beauty of a small patio is that it costs less to install and decorate using the best materials and most costly accessories. If the area is very cramped, it can even be made to look bigger than it really is by using mirrors, fake

15

doorways, white paint and *trompe l'œil* effects (*see* page 88). It seems that limited space only encourages an inventive approach with exciting and enjoyable results.

It is the large patio that appears to present design problems. A vast area of unrelieved paving with a few containers around the edges tends to look rather barren and bleak. It can be difficult to know how to fill that space when your patio furniture looks a little lost and you can't really afford any more expensive tubs and containers. If you are planning a patio of significant proportions, it is important to incorporate plenty of variety into your design. Breaking up the area, even visually with different paving materials arranged in blocks, strips and patterns, immediately adds interest and disguises the size and shape of the site. Some materials are particularly complementary, such as a pattern or border of coloured bricks to liven up plain paving slabs. Other combinations are useful for making changes of texture, just as you would when designing an interior room. Areas of some rough textured material like gravel or cobbles may not be as practical for standing furniture or plant containers, but in a large patio scheme, they are useful for their visual effect or for designating an area that you don't want to be walked across. Leaving planned spaces in the paving for planting beds is another effective way of breaking up the main area. These can be used to divide the patio into smaller areas and planted with larger plants, shrubs and trees to create screens and windbreaks, or filled with bright seasonal blooms purely for their decorative effect. Beds can be bordered in matching paving materials or raised using brick, stone or timber to produce extra height and interest. This is a good treatment if

Fig II   Steps and walling will integrate the patio area neatly with the rest of the garden.

*Fig 12   Timber decking makes an attractive and easy-to-install patio surface, especially where you might like to incorporate built-in plant containers and changes in level.*

the patio is going to be used by anyone confined to a wheelchair.

Another way to add interest and variety to a large area is to introduce changes of level and these can be successfully designed in matching or contrasting paving materials. The different areas can be linked by steps or gentle slopes and raised areas of various sizes and shapes. These changes of levels can be used as sunbathing platforms, plant display beds, built-in seating, handy garden storage for toys, tools, cushions or other accessories (with lift-up wooden tops) or, most successfully, a sequence of formal pools linked by small waterfalls, fountains or weirs. A large patio serving several purposes benefits from being divided into more distinct separate garden 'rooms' using screens, large plants and pergolas to create a complete and highly sophisticated patio complex. This might include a sunny sun terrace for lounging, with a shadier area tucked behind for dining in comfort, a sheltered

children's play area complete with sand-pit, paddling pool and other outdoor games, even a private corner fitted with an outdoor hot tub or spa.

When planning the total shape of your patio, there is no reason, other than that of habit and convention, why it should be the familiar square or rectangular design, although this does make calculating paving materials easier. Sometimes available space limits you to certain dimensions or creating an L-shape or more irregular pattern. This makes sense in order to incorporate a large immoveable feature or irregularly shaped site. Within these limitations, you can usually afford to be a little more creative if you are keen to stamp originality and character into your patio design. An irregular shape may be designed to interlock with other features such as a formal pool or planting beds; however, paving need not meet the lawn or garden in a straight line, as slabs and pavers could be arranged diagonally and

17

extended to create a zigzag or scalloped edge. You also could blur the edges of your hard surface with creeping ground-cover plants, allowing the patio to merge gradually with the rest of the garden, perhaps blended into a path or stepping stones and creating no definite formal shape.

Sometimes an ornamental paving range will suggest an interesting shape or design: interlocking shapes can be used to create hexagons, circles and other formal geometric designs, which are particularly suited to a central patio where they can radiate out from your central feature. Remember too, that circles need not be complete and free-standing: if you enjoy juggling with shapes and patterns, semicircles, snaking curves and other modifications can be incorporated into more straight-edged shapes to introduce softer profiles into your garden design — all straight lines can look rather rigid and dull.

## PRACTICAL POINTS TO CONSIDER

Creative ideas and imaginative plans are all very well, but your patio plan must be practical and affordable as well as exciting to look at. Double check your ideas on paper to make sure they are not going to be too complicated to construct or that it will not work out too costly to buy the materials. There are various practical points to consider in actual construction. Where the patio is to be sited behind a terraced, linked or semi-detached property, on a balcony or roof space, limited access may cause you to alter your plans if heavy materials have to be taken through the house. Delivery and storage of bulky items may also be a problem, if you are constructing a patio in an already established garden which you'd like to remain relatively undisturbed and undamaged. It pays to work out exactly where, how and when such items are going to be handled before you order the ready-mix concrete or a couple of tons of slabs. You may have to change your plans or enlist the co-operation of your neighbours to make it work.

Other practical points you may not have considered could cause you problems or extra expense once you start constructing your patio area. A sloping site must be levelled or terraced if you wish to pave it and this will involve expensive and time-consuming levelling and backfilling. It may be more sensible to choose another site or to consider a raised timber-decked surface which is by far the cheapest and easiest way to cope with slopes and unwanted changes in level. Flexible decking can be used to level a site or be constructed on different levels incorporating simply-made built-in wooden seating and other features. You may also have to consider existing drains and inspection covers which may need to be moved if they are not to spoil your patio design. And, where the area butts up to the house or other building, check that the new level does not breach the damp-proof course. Privacy is another practical point that may be forgotten in the excitement of incorporating all the features and facilities you want for your patio. This is particularly important where you are planning a sunbathing or dining area and don't want to be overlooked by neighbours or passers-by. Adequate screening will have to be allowed for and if you are intending to use shrubs or climbing plants as a living curtain, you may have to erect a more immediate, temporary fence or screen until the plants have grown.

## PATIO STYLE

Because most patios are strongly defined in shape and size — often on three sides by screening or by the wall of an adjoining building — and include a lot of hard-surfaced materials, they tend to be naturally formal in style which often suits their role as an extension of the home and sophisticated outdoor living/dining room. However, it is possible to create a more informal atmosphere, if that would suit your home and lifestyle better. By choosing second-hand materials, such as real stone slabs or matured timbers, and softening them with climbing and creeping plants, you have the framework for a woodland style or wild plant patio. This could include a small pond, a rustic seat, areas of bark chips and other natural features that would quickly attract a wide variety of insects and birds for your contemplation.

Nor is there any reason why you should not design a cottage-style patio based on the traditional cottage garden. This always has a shaggy, rather informal air with old-fashioned plants such as pinks, rambling roses, hollyhocks, honeysuckle and Sweet Williams which have been allowed to go a little mad and smother every surface. Many of these can easily be grown in tubs or containers or in special patio beds to create the same look on the patio, with old flagstones or cobbles used to produce the right effect underfoot. Suitably rustic or traditional-style seating and simple wooden barrels for your plants should complete the chocolate-box rural atmosphere.

Because most patios are well sheltered and positioned where they will catch maximum sunshine, they can enjoy temperatures far in excess of the rest of the garden. This favourable microclimate can be profitably exploited to create a wonderfully scented and relaxing Mediterranean atmosphere, with a miniature container-grown kitchen garden for more tender, difficult-to-grow fruits and vegetables such as peppers, aubergines and kiwi fruits (a most useful patio climber even if the climate is not warm enough to encourage it to fruit). The Mediterranean-style patio will flourish in a dry, scorching sun-trap if you select the right kind of plants. Often grey-leaved or fleshy-foliaged, these oil-rich herbs and flowers will release a wonderful scent in full sunshine and are ideal for growing in tubs, as most prefer a dry, stony soil. A bright umbrella, terracotta pots for your plants and a barbecue in the corner should be enough to conjure up the relaxing pleasures of sunny days spent abroad.

You can also use the patio's sheltered climate to create a jungle effect of exotic subtropical and dramatic architectural plants with huge or strangely shaped and marked foliage. This is a look that can be wildly informal or as semi-formal

Fig 13 A colour co-ordinated patio where the choice of flowers has been limited to a sophisticated blend of white and pastel shades, against a background of dark green foliage.

as a Victorian glasshouse, depending on how the plants are contained and controlled. Really tender species can be brought undercover in winter to maintain a lush, exotic display.

If you do choose to go for a more formal style, your choice of plants and materials will again control the look and move towards the oriental, the hi tech or city slickness.

For a more traditional style, you can choose Regency, Victorian or other antique features, which may be selected to match the architecture of your home. Metal, concrete and Perspex are uncompromisingly modern, although they can be softened in some cases by carefully positioned plants. However, when they are used to create features such as furniture, sculpture and screens, and combined with dramatic foliage plants, the effect is smart and stylish and offers the opportunity to experiment with unusual shapes and painted colours.

The oriental garden or patio may be equally stark and simple in its planning, but it is essentially designed to provide a relaxing, anti-stress environment. Natural materials, such as rock, stone, sand and water, play an important role, arranged in imitation of natural features such as lakes, hills and forests to create a miniature landscape. Plants tend to be kept to a minimum and are restricted to tightly clipped or controlled evergreens in order to produce the correct sculpted effect. Shrubs and bushes like ornamental cherries, Japanese maples, rhododendrons and azaleas can be used to provide a

special seasonal blaze of colour and interest. Dwarf varieties of these plants make it possible to grow them in containers or special beds on the patio. Other plants, such as bamboo, have a decided oriental air and will grow well in a pot or tub. In the garden, it tends to be rather too invasive, but restricted to a large oriental glazed urn it looks superb and offers a wide range of interesting striped, speckled and coloured stem effects. Like the Mediterranean garden, this is a style that adapts very well to the patio, since both have a strong tradition of courtyard gardening.

Unless you are deliberately aiming at a complete contrast of style, such as an enclosed patio area with a distinctive look or character of its own, which is intended as a special kind of retreat or surprise feature, the patio usually will be influenced by the style of building or garden it adjoins. For the country cottage or town house,

*Fig 14 A dramatic two-level patio with a strong oriental flavour.*

patio features and plants can be chosen to fully co-ordinate and make the transition between inside and outside as smooth as possible. Matching brick, stone or timber to other features such as the house, an outbuilding, trellis or pergola, also helps this new area blend in immediately. If you are hoping for an old-fashioned, mellow look, second-hand materials will give an instant impression of maturity especially once mosses and climbing plants have started to grow and soften the outline of structural features.

Another starting point for your patio design, might be a paving range that catches your imagination, and there are a great many colours and shapes that can be fitted together in an infinite variety of patterns and designs (see page 29). However, it might be a single feature or accessory that sparks off the imagination and sets a specially styled theme – this could be an interesting pot picked up on a holiday abroad, a collection of favourite plants or a small ornamental fountain. Any idea can be successfully expanded and adapted into a full-scale patio scheme to suit any size or location.

## GENERAL DESIGN TIPS

You probably have some idea of how you want your patio to look regarding style and size, but choosing the individual features and functions can be difficult, particularly where there isn't a lot of space and you haven't room for everything you fancy. It helps to sit down right at the beginning and think carefully what purpose do you want the patio to serve, how you will use it and which features will give you most pleasure. If you make a list, it will make it easier to assess the amount of space required for each one, before you decide which should take priority and judge where any can be neatly linked or amalgamated. It may be that plants will take priority on your patio, or that you have set your heart on an elaborate water feature, and seating will simply be incorporated in the scheme or positioned where these features can be best enjoyed.

Others may want to plan the patio as an outdoor dining room for entertaining friends, complete with comfortable chairs and table, sophisticated barbecue facilities, good lighting for evening meals and adequate shade from the midday sun. Here plants will take a secondary place, acting as a mere backdrop of scents and colours to the soft furnishings. For the family garden, a children's play area may be most important, with a sensible trestle or picnic table for family meals and which can be left out all year. It is worth considering at this stage, where you are going to store all those patio accessories that are not tough enough to withstand winter weather: if there is no room in the garden shed or garage, you may have to find space for a small storage box or building in your plans. If you are keen to grow tender edibles, there will be room to find for your growbags or even a mini lean-to greenhouse or frame which can be positioned against the house wall. It all takes up space, but if you work out carefully what you'd like and are prepared to play around with your plans on paper, you'll be surprised what can be neatly fitted in. A formal layout lends itself to interlocking, dual-purpose and back-to-back features which if well planned, can look as stylish as they are practical.

Drawing up your patio ideas to scale on paper goes a long way towards seeing if your plans will work and can show where you might have to compromise. It is also invaluable for calculating the materials you need, which is essential if you are keen to devise a complicated paving pattern. However, it is equally important to get some impression of how your ideas will work in practice, before ordering costly materials or beginning complicated construction work. You can mark out the area with pegs and string, and use empty cardboard boxes, lengths of hosepipe and strips of old carpet to show where major features will be positioned. This is invaluable for seeing how features might work together, whether they are of the correct scale and generally how the plan hangs together as a whole. It helps to be able to view your rough layout from various obvious vantage points: from the house and the rest of the garden (checking from an upstairs window is always useful to see the plan in perspective). This technique also allows you to alter and amend your plans easily.

## PLANNING FOR THE SEASONS

Most patios serve a variety of functions and will expect to be used most of the year. Even when the weather isn't fine enough to venture out-doors, the area is often on view from the house so needs to look its best right through the seasons. This need not involve tedious maintenance or excessive care, providing a good strong framework of structural features and perennial plants is installed right from the beginning. Small shrubs, even trees and climbing, creeping and architectural evergreens should form the backbone of your scheme, softening and livening a good basic design of hard landscaping materials such as paving, walls, screens and fences. Something of interest for each season can be added to this basic layout. This might take the

*Fig 15  Experiment with different colour combinations; here yellow and mauve blooms look superb against a background of dark green foliage.*

form of a shrub or perennial plant that blooms at a particular time of year or seasonal plants which are quickly and easily added and replaced as and when they are required and need very little maintenance.

## Winter

Too many patios are neglected in winter, yet with a little forethought and care, they can offer just as much visual pleasure as any other season. Firstly, it is important to make sure that the area is tidy at the end of the summer, clearing pots and containers of annual bedding plants after the first frosts, keeping leaves swept before they sink into a soggy, unsightly mess, and doing any necessary tidying and pruning jobs – this need not take more than an hour or so of your time. Evergreen plants should maintain life, colour and interest through the colder months and prevent the area looking too bleak – although the sight of a statue, lonely clipped evergreen bush or craggy rock starkly half buried in snow can be breath-taking. You should aim to have something at all levels, including ground-cover plants as well as taller shrubs or trees and climbers for interest above eye level. There are plants that are at their best in winter and one or two of these will put on a wonderfully unexpected display when the rest of the garden is dormant, such as a winter-flowering jasmine which is ideal to train over a patio trellis or screen. There is a surprisingly wide variety of plants that bloom in winter, many of them beautifully scented, which only adds to the unexpected pleasure should the weather allow you outside. Non weather-proof garden furniture should be brought inside over winter but it is useful to have some kind of seat such as a sturdy garden bench or even a built-in seat, where you can sit and view the garden for five minutes on finer days.

## Spring

Tubs and containers are perfect for an early display of spring bulbs, as their brilliant colours and freshness are a welcome sight from the house in the first real sunshine of the year; and their massed effect is a pleasure to observe and scent as the garden begins to warm up. Patio pots offer the opportunity to plan some exciting combinations and effects, by contrasting different shapes, co-ordinating colours, and trying out new varieties each year. Bulbs are usually planted in autumn when they can replace the last flowering summer annuals; remove them when they are past their best and replace them with new summer plants, in early summer or late spring. Many shrubs and climbers can also be relied on to produce a fine spring display of blooms: different varieties of clematis alone can be planned to bloom from the earliest months right through to midsummer and are perfect for smothering patio trellises and fences with quick growing foliage and flowers.

## Summer

Unless the scheme is intended to be a sophisticated all-green exotic or oriental theme, the summer months on the patio are for free-flowering annuals planted in tubs, containers, raised beds, and hanging baskets. Like spring bulbs, combining different colours and effects can be great fun especially as there is even more choice and variety among bedding plants. These range from low-growing carpet, cushion and trailing plants to giant blooms, as well as varieties that produce a mass of flowers over a long season, and every shade and colour imaginable from brilliant hot reds, oranges and yellows to softer pastel pinks, blues and creams. New combinations can be planned each year, giving you the perfect opportunity to experiment with contrasting and co-ordinated effects. If you don't find the gaudy effect of mixing too many bright colours very relaxing, or you are trying to encourage a sophisticated more low-key patio scheme, consider a single or dual colour theme, such as blues and mauves or all white or yellows and creams, which can often look extremely stunning.

## Autumn

Autumn can be a difficult season on the patio. Summer flowers will be dying back, and you will be wanting to tidy up and get ready for winter, as well as clear containers in order to plant your bulbs for spring. However, there are summer bedding plants that will keep going until after the first hard frosts, and late-flowering species like chrysanthemums are useful for adding a splash of autumn colour to your evergreen framework. There are some shrubs and climbers whose dying foliage can be relied on to produce a brilliant splash of gold or russet colour and it may be worth including one or two of these in your initial plans – a dwarf Japanese maple in a suitably oriental pot, a Virginia creeper, encouraged to smother the wall of the house or a shrubby witch hazel which may not only produce red or yellow autumn foliage, but flowers prettily along its bare branches in winter. Plants producing berries are also useful for adding a flash of warm colour in autumn and if the birds leave them alone, they will last well into winter too. A low-growing cotoneaster with its glossy green leaves and bright berries is a useful shrub for the townhouse or roof-garden patio, since it is tough and resistant to pollution.

# PLANNING FOR AFTER DARK

Some form of outdoor lighting is essential for the patio if you want to extend its use after dark, as it provides the opportunity to sit out and enjoy the garden on balmy nights, to eat your evening meals outside or throw full-scale parties and barbecues for your friends. Often lighting a good-looking patio area will make a fine view from the house even when the weather isn't warm enough to sit outside, and this can be a real asset to a dining room or living room with large picture windows or patio doors. There are also important safety and security benefits in being able to light the area immediately outside the house, making it worthwhile to plan for indoor

23

*Fig 16  Garden lights mean the patio can be used and enjoyed at night, as well as when the sun shines.*

switches. Not only will lights deter intruders, you will be able to see your way around should you need to go outside.

Patio lighting is best planned at the earliest stages as a complete system. This way you can work out exactly the type of lighting you need and where you'll need it, and then be able to conceal wires and cables neatly out of site within the actual patio construction. All cables for exterior use should be protected by a special plastic conduit and buried to a depth of at least 46cm (18in). If your patio is already installed, or the majority of the structural work has been com-

pleted, outdoor electrics can still be added but cables will have to be pegged out of reach along the top of walls and fences using special fixing clips. Sometimes the cable can be tucked into the mortar pointing of a wall where it will be slightly recessed. Unless you have experience of working with electricity it is advisable to enlist the help of a qualified electrician. You should only use fitments and accessories recommended for outdoor use and the total system should be fitted with an RCB safety circuit breaker which cuts off the power automatically should there be any deviation in the current. Light fittings can vary from between 150–300w, and it is important to realise that there is a limit to the number and size of lights you can run from a single cable and that this capacity is also affected by the distance the cable has to run from the house. Power levels drop quite considerably over long distances and a thicker cable or several of them may be required to cope with the extra load. It may be that you would like to extend your lights to the rest of the garden, highlighting particular plants and features or simply lighting paths and drives for safety and convenience. Another point to consider when assessing outdoor electrics is whether you will be installing any pools or moving water features such as fountains and cascades (see page 78), as the total capacity for running pumps and filters will have to be added to your calculations.

There are a great many different kinds of outdoor lights and effects and if you are hoping to use your patio extensively, it is well worth planning in advance exactly which you need and putting them together as a complete system as carefully as you would for any interior room. A sophisticated mixture of effects is best rather than relying on one or two bright lights to illuminate the area rather harshly. This softer lighting can be a combination of uplighters, downlighters and spots which will still produce the same light levels but more subtly, making a far more comfortable and enjoyable environment. Ideally, it should be possible to operate different lights separately so that you can vary the effect.

If you are planning a sophisticated patio scheme, beware of coloured light bulbs – although the blue and green bulbs are sometimes useful for highlighting foliage – a mixture of reds and yellows can look quite garish producing a fairy grotto effect. However, this garish effect can be quite fun for parties and bulbs can always be changed for special occasions.

## Types and Effects

Garden lights are generally available in one of three types, each of which produces a different effect; tungsten which makes a warm, yellow light, discharge lighting which has more of a cold, blue-green tinge (particularly suitable for illuminating water and plants), and low voltage tungsten halogen lights of which the clear white light reveals the true natural colours of flowers, foliage and features. These all require a transformer but several lights can be run from the one unit.

You can choose a variety of fitments, including simple spotlights which come on a long spike and can be hidden in tubs and containers or planting beds to shine up through the foliage to soften any glare. Alternatively, these can be fitted to walls, fences, buildings, a pergola and even trees to act as downlighters, so long as care is taken to angle the light or filter the glare through leaves to avoid being dazzled. These can be used not only to highlight individual plants, but to highlight any special feature such as a statue, piece of sculpture or archway. You will also need good but comfortable lighting over the barbecue and dining areas to avoid struggling with food in the shadows, and again, you must be careful to angle the spotlights so that they are not too glaring.

Floodlights produce more of a widespread

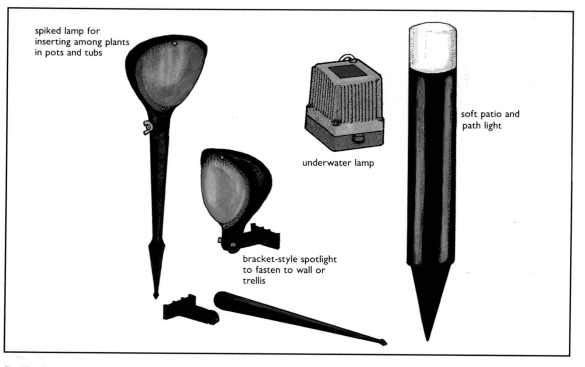

spiked lamp for inserting among plants in pots and tubs

underwater lamp

bracket-style spotlight to fasten to wall or trellis

soft patio and path light

Fig 17   Outdoor lamps and lanterns not only enable the patio area to be used after the sun has set, they also can produce wonderful visual effects to be enjoyed from house or garden.

25

run from the same power source you are using for pumps and filters. There is even a range of combined fountain and light fitments which are useful for small pools.

Some lights are designed to be on show rather than hidden away: weatherproof bulkhead lights are popular for attaching to walls and produce a good, non-glare light. But there are also ground and wall-mounted lanterns in both modern and traditional styles which are useful for lighting paths, the patio perimeters, and walls, and can be paired either side of steps or entrances. Free-standing lanterns can be low to the ground or quite a few feet tall, imitating the style of the old street lamps and being useful for producing a higher level light where the patio is lacking a pergola or any overhead structure. For parties and special occasions, it can be fun to string up rows of coloured fairy lights.

A combination of several types of light can produce some interesting and exciting effects. A combination of foreground and background lighting generates a complete three-dimensional effect. It is particularly attractive to create a 'moonlight' effect by shining light through foliage from both above and below, making dappled patterns. If you are looking to illuminate a pool and don't want to install underwater lighting, do not shine spotlights directly on the water, it is too glaring; instead, highlight surrounding features so that their reflection is softly illuminated. It is wonderful to be able to produce all these effects at the touch of a switch, but non-electric lights have their place on the patio too. Nightlights, candles and wax or paraffin lanterns are softly romantic for summer meals or special occasions such as a party. Candles can be popped into glass jars and stood on the table or hung from strings or the pergola overhead. A few candles spread around the patio is often a good idea in any case, once dusk begins to fall, as many are specially treated to deter insects. Spiked flares can also be used for special occasions, as they can be lit and inserted in containers or flower beds. Some of these are made from bamboo and filled with oil so are reusable.

Fig 18  Wall-mounted lanterns are both smart and practical.

light and are equally useful for washing a larger area with light or to wash the wall of a building. This can look particularly effective where your house has interesting architectural features because when these features are thrown into relief, they make an attractive backdrop.

There is another type of uplighter called a wall light which is sunk unobtrusively in the ground. Set on a bed of gravel for good drainage and covered with toughened safety glass or a special grid, these can be buried in the main patio structure to provide an unobtrusive light source.

There is also a wide range of light fitments suitable for pools and fountains. Low voltage underwater lamps and spotlights can often be

CHAPTER 3

# Choosing Materials and Laying the Patio

If you have chosen the site, shape and size of your new patio and are satisfied that it is going to look right in respect to both your house and garden, you are ready to start planning the details. This planning will include making your choice of paving materials and getting started on the actual construction. If the choices available and the work involved seem a little daunting, it may help to consider exactly how you are going to use the patio. This will influence the type of hard surface you require underfoot and ultimately the general look of the patio. It will also help assess whether you are spending your budget sensibly. Do you just want a practical hard surface area for the children to play on, where you can keep an eye on them from the house, with room for a few pieces of inexpensive patio furniture so that you can also sit out on sunny days? Or is the area

*Fig 19   Pre-formed paving slabs in imitation of natural York stone.*

destined to be part of a much larger garden design, contributing splashes of colours, interesting plants and specially designed areas of shade and sun for dining and lounging? Do you want the patio to blend completely with the house as well as the garden, in which case you will have to select materials that combine elements of both areas. In fact, it may be necessary to find suitable second-hand materials to achieve a properly aged or mellow look to be in keeping with both house and garden. Then again, you may be planning a stylish outdoor room – truly an extension of the house where you will be entertaining family and friends in style.

Once you have a clear idea of the practical and decorative functions of your proposed patio, you will find it easier to decide which paving materials will be most suitable for your requirements. For

*Fig 20 Hexagonal pavers are cleverly infilled with small stones to great decorative effect.*

instance, if you are looking for just a basic, inexpensive surface that will serve as a play area and a practical hard surface for a table and chairs, a continuous paved area using prefabricated concrete slabs is probably the cheapest and quickest option to install. It can always be livened up during the summer months with inexpensive tubs of quick-growing summer annuals, guaranteed to put on a good show for a relatively small investment of time and money. However, if you are trying to create an instantly mellow effect that will blend well with the garden and look as though it has been there for years, then far more expensive materials such as natural stone or old brick which will look good against the house, are preferable. If instead of putting mortar between them you fill the gaps with soil and plant low-growing, ground-cover plants like thyme, that don't mind being trodden on, this will help soften any hard edges and quickly produce a more mature, informal look.

Another factor that may influence your choice of materials is the shapes and patterns you have planned for your patio. For instance, a circular or semicircular area looks good laid with bricks or small paviors. Any other features you hope to include like a raised pool, or built-in beds may also help you decide whether you want the paved area to match. An excellent alternative for a great many situations is low-level timber decking; it looks very natural, is easy to install and can incorporate an infinite variety of other features such as planting beds, furniture, changes in level or even a formal pool.

Of course taste, style and personal preferences are going to sway your final decision as much as anything and there are so many different styles to choose from it should be possible to satisfy all tastes and budgets. At least, being aware of some of the practical advantages and disadvantages of different materials and how they might meet your specific needs, will give a better idea of whether you are making the right decision. Whether you are aiming at a harmonious scheme to blend with house and garden, or a striking contrast to stimulate and excite, you will have to live with the final effect, so it is sensible to satisfy your needs when making that final choice. These pointers are simply a guide that will hopefully prevent you making any expensive or unnecessary mistakes.

## FLOORING MATERIALS

There are two main types of hard surface paving materials; firstly, there is unit paving including bricks, paving slabs, stone setts, and natural stone. Then there is continuous paving; this refers to an undivided stretch of mixed granular materials such as concrete or shingle. Whichever you choose, it is important to remember — particularly with certain unit materials, like bricks and tiles — to check they are recommended for outdoor use and are of the right type to withstand the effects of frost and rain. Porous bricks, for example, may flake or crack in a severe frost.

Looking in more detail at the individual types, you can see each has its practical and decorative advantages.

## Concrete

Concrete is a popular and flexible patio surface for the modern home. In its plainest form, it tends to look rather bleak over large areas and suffers from excessive glare on very sunny days. However, concrete can be coloured by mixing in proprietary colouring powders at the preparation stage. To achieve a more interesting textured appearance, you lightly brush the surface of the concrete while it is still wet, which should expose the aggregate. Another method involves brushing the surface with a soft broom about six to eight hours after laying and then hosing it down. There are also concrete pattern 'stamps', which, if applied to the stretch of concrete while still wet, reproduce the divided effect of different paving designs. If you still think this is not exciting enough, you could apply stone, marble chippings or fine shingle to the wet surface, to produce a

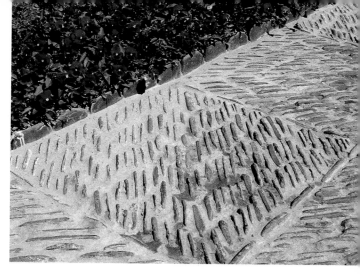

Fig 21 Flat stones stuck into the wet cement has produced interesting patterns and textures — the same principle as cobbles but with a more modern appearance.

speckled mosaic effect. Another alternative is to mark out and divide areas of concrete with lines of bricks to create patterns. This would be an excellent way of linking the patio boundary with a lawn or a pool or to divide a large area into smaller sections.

## Bricks

Areas of brick look very attractive in informal or cottage gardens, particularly if you can find a sufficient supply of old bricks. These are often available from salvage yards, although they tend to be no cheaper than new ones. New bricks, which come in a surprisingly wide range of colours from sandy yellow through the reds and oranges to black, can also be used to good effect around modern buildings. However, only use the special hard paving bricks or stock bricks for patio use.

You can experiment using different shades and colours to create interesting patterns and designs. One of the exciting aspects of using brick as a paving material is all the different design patterns you can devise. For instance, bricks can be laid in basketweave or herringbone designs, or staggered in the same way as bricks are laid in a wall. They are best loosely laid — flat rather than on edge — and leaving a joint of about 1cm (⅜in) between each one, which can be filled with sand.

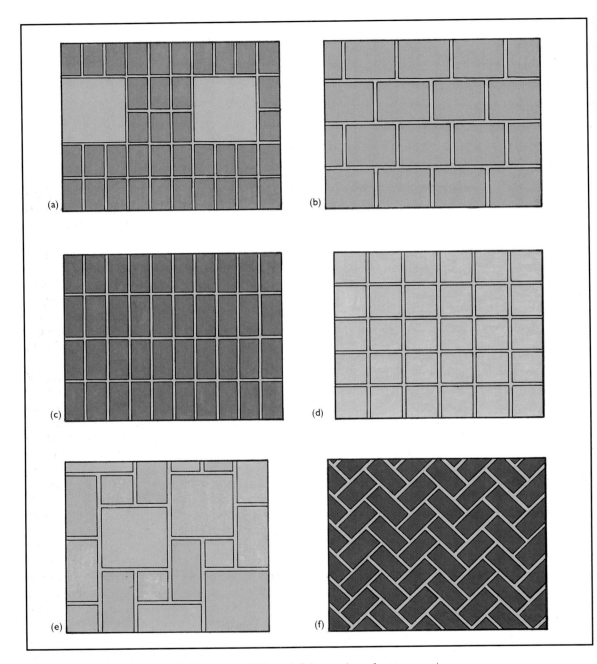

Fig 22  Paving slabs, stones and bricks can be laid in an infinite number of patterns and designs to maintain interest and originality: (a) mixing concrete slabs with bricks; (b) staggering the joints when laying plain paving slabs to make them more interesting; (c) Mediterranean terracotta tiles; (d) square concrete pavers; (e) different sizes, shapes and colours produce a crazy paving effect; (f) bricks or blocks laid in a herringbone pattern.

Fig 23 *Bricks can be laid in a wide range of attractive patterns and designs, producing mellow variations of colour and shade.*

Fig 24 *Simple timber decking can be laid down in a great many stylish and elaborate designs.*

You should also remember that if the patio is going to be well used, the bricks will need a deeper hardcore than paving slabs, because the larger size of the slab helps distribute the weight when it is walked upon. The depth of hardcore for bricks should therefore be at least 15cm (6in).

## Timber Decking

Timber decking comprises low-level timber planks arranged in strips or patterns to form a continuous decking surface. It is usually raised a few inches off the ground and supported on wooden posts or joists, or fastened to the wall with sturdy coach bolts when the patio adjoins the house or another building. Where the site demands it, the platform can be raised to any level, providing the supporting structure is suitably strengthened. Timber decking is also available in pre-finished square sections just a couple of inches high, which can be laid just like paving slabs except that they require no fixing. These are an excellent idea where you might require a temporary surface as a cover up, or where you are looking for a lightweight, easy-to-install material such as on a balcony or a roof-top patio. Decking more than 45cm (18in) off the ground should always be fitted with a safety rail.

Timber decking is reasonably simple to construct and wonderfully flexible, in that it can be fitted around almost any size and shape and neatly integrated with other features such as platforms, furniture and units with lift-up lids. It also has a fine natural appearance that seems to harmonize with both structural materials and the more natural soft landscaping aspects of the garden, such as plants. It can also adopt almost any style and appearance from a smooth, cool, bleached look for the modern home, to rough and ready recycled timbers for a more rustic-style patio, and therefore, can be adapted to suit almost any situation. It really comes into its own on a practical level however, with a sloping or very uneven site, where the construction of a conventional concrete patio would involve making a large retaining wall and then backfilling to provide a level surface for paving.

There are various kinds of timber suitable for decking from tough Western red cedar or chestnut (which are particularly excellent for outdoor use being easy to maintain and slow to rot), to inexpensive deal or pine. Softwoods can be used as surface timbers provided they are thoroughly treated with preservative on an annual basis. Both hard and soft timbers should be scoured with a rough brush every spring to prevent them becoming dangerously slippery with fungal growth.

Stains and varnishes can be used to maintain a wide range of natural effects. Timber can be bleached white or grey to produce an antique weathered appearance, or tinted blue, green or red for more exciting results. The depth of colour is controlled by the number of treatments applied. Decking not only offers an exciting choice of colour and grain options like brick, but it can also be laid in a variety of decorative patterns such as herringbone and weave. When laid in blocks with the planks facing in different directions or on the diagonal, the timbers can be used

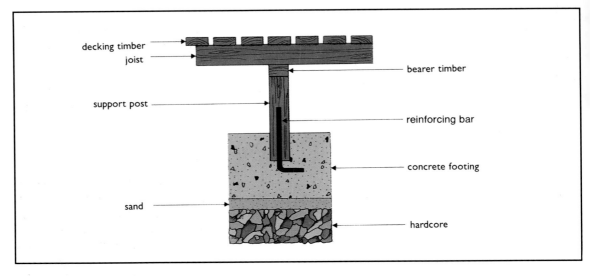

Fig 25 *Low-level decks can be supported by timber posts, driven into metal-fencing spikes or fixed in concrete footings using a reinforcing bar as a dowel. The posts should be spanned by bearer timbers.*

to create some interesting optical illusions, which are useful for disguising the real shape and size of a less than perfect patio site.

## Natural Stone

Sandstone and limestone are the most popular types of natural stone available for garden use. They are available as square paving slabs with a textured surface, and as random stone slabs for use as 'crazy paving'. In the latter case wide joints are created and filled with soil, then you can plant carpet- and cushion-forming plants, such as creeping thymes and tough alpine species.

Marble is attractive (and very expensive), but its cool appearance does not lend itself to the generally wet climate of Northern Europe. The best setting for marble would be a small city courtyard type of garden. If you use marble, it should have a honed anti-slip surface for safety.

## Paving Slabs

Preformed slabs are the most common form of patio paving and are ideal for a patio around a

modern house. Although made of concrete, they come in various shapes and sizes, such as square, rectangular or hexagonal, some of which can be put together in a variety of interlocking designs. This variety, together with a wide range of colours, textures and styles, gives you plenty of choice. In particular, there are various types of specially textured surfaces available, often imitating natural stone or brick. Some of the more expensive types are remarkably realistic and yet still considerably cheaper than the real thing. Most concrete pavers are recommended as being antislip when wet for safety purposes.

## Tiles

Quarry tiles can also be used outside, providing winter conditions are not too severe, and the heather-coloured ones can look particularly attractive. Their smoother, sleeker appearance is suited to a more sophisticated setting, particularly if the patio opens directly off a conservatory, kitchen or similar room with matching flooring. They are also well suited to the balcony or roof patio. Ceramic tiles offer an infinite variety of

Fig 26 An essentially Japanese-style patio, employing a timber walkway across areas of gravel and pebbles.

patterns, colours and designs, and can be used both to create a Mediterranean flavour on a small sheltered patio or roof-top terrace, or to make a superb sleek surface around a swimming-pool. Tiles used outdoors must be recommended as frost and slip resistant.

## Gravel and Shingle

This may not seem like the ideal material to have on a patio since it is not particularly stable for furniture nor comfortable underfoot. However, it mixes well visually with other surfaces if confined to well defined areas, that are designed to add variety and interest, and it will break up the monotony of one material spread over a large area. It looks particularly pleasing when used to divide artificial slabs by providing an interesting variation in texture, and because it provides excellent drainage, such areas are ideal for standing pots and containers.

Pea shingle is often used as an occasional patio surface and should be applied at least 2.5cm (1in) thick. A gravel area on your patio may need confining by edging the area with partially buried wooden boards, or by a brick surround.

## Cobbles

This is another material that may seem unsuitable for a patio or terrace but, like gravel, if it is used as a mixing material it can provide attractive areas, especially round large containers, or as a border area next to a wall. Don't forget that the cobbles, although simple to lay, will have to

be packed together as close as possible in a bed of mortar or concrete, on a hardcore base, so keep the area to be cobbled to a practical size. Alternatively, you could lay them on a dry bed of mortar or concrete and water them in with a sprinkler. Cobbles are also available as square setts which are laid in the same manner as paving slabs.

## Stone and Granite Setts

Interesting and unusual effects can be created by using these less conventional paving materials. These setts are usually about 13 or 25sq cm (5 or 10sq in) and are more usually employed in road construction. However, bought second-hand they make an excellent and hard-wearing surface that has a surprisingly mellow appearance. And you can lay them in patterns or use them in conjunction with smaller, unit paving.

### Mixing and Matching

When you look in more detail at the different styles of material available, you can appreciate that mixing materials on the patio is nothing to

Fig 27 An interesting edging treatment where the ground slopes away, combining old sleepers and boulders.

*Fig 28 Slices of timber used as a paving material form a fine contrast to an adjoining gravel area.*

be afraid of. And if you take care when choosing and positioning – the proportion of one to another and the shapes of the different areas have to be right – the combination can create a far more varied and exciting look. Other good mixing ideas include brick edging, which can be used to separate concrete paving slabs into an attractive chequer-board design. Timber decking butted on to a harder, stone surface can be used to denote a change of area and a complete contrast of texture. If your patio runs down to a pool or larger stretch of water, you could edge if off with old railway sleepers sunk into the ground and then have a small pebble beach down to the water. The timbers could be staggered or laid to a formal edge. The possibilities are endless, once you explore the options and put your imagination to work.

## BUILDING THE PATIO

Once the site has been chosen and the desired materials purchased, you will be anxious for the actual laying of the patio to begin and for your ideas to take shape.

### Design

Accuracy is essential if you want to construct your patio successfully, and it helps to begin by drawing a scale plan, marking all the lines of drains, positions of manhole covers and water pipes, and to note the areas within or immediately bordering the patio where you wish to make plantings. This drawing should be representative of a unit of measurement on the ground, using a suggested scale of lcm : 50cm (lin : 4ft). This technique gives you the opportunity to plan to the finest degree. Use squared paper that suits the scale you are working to and draw in your ideas on tracing paper. Leave some time before transferring to the main plan, as this will give you the opportunity to change your mind and alter the layout. When you have made up your mind, you should transfer to the proper scale drawing, adding colour where it might help distinguish one type of surface from another; even subtle colour changes or patterning will help you establish and recognize variations in height and so on. Using this method, you should be able to get some impression of what your patio plan will look like in three-dimensional terms.

Next, using manufacturers' plans and leaflets, you can work out an appropriate layout using standard sizes, and this will avoid having to cut too many slabs or bricks. If the site is to be terraced, there must be provision for steps, ramps and retaining walls.

Manhole covers present a problem because it is against building regulations to cover them over completely. If you are lucky enough to be planning the patio before the drains are laid, ask that the manholes are sited to suit you. Otherwise a manhole can be disguised by placing a plant container or training a creeping plant over it, to be pushed back when needed. It is possible to use a special recessed manhole cover, into the top of which an appropriately cut paving can be fixed. Alternatively, the height of the manhole cover can be adjusted to suit the patio level by adding or removing a layer of bricks within the inspection chamber. If none of these alternatives are possible you may have to relay the drains in a more convenient position. If you do this the local building inspector will have to be informed.

# Building a Basic Patio with Concrete Slabs

Start by clearing the site of the top soil and making it roughly level. Remember at this stage, that if the patio is adjoining the house the finished level must be not less than 15cm (6in) below the house damp-proof course. Also you should never cover up a house air vent. Houses built before the mid-twentieth century have damp-proof courses very close to the ground, and paving laid immediately under such a low course will crack at the joint between it and the house. This cracking results from the subsoil expanding and contracting with differences in humidity. Moss will germinate in the crack and bridge the damp-proof course, producing a damp interior wall.

This can be solved in the following way: after excavating, stand an old floorboard or plank about 2cm (⅞in) thick on edge on the footings and pave up to that. This leaves an inch-wide channel which can be cleaned out like a gutter twice a year.

It is also worth remembering at this stage, that if you have the other end of the patio abutting the lawn, to set the slabs below the level of the lawn. Either 1–1.2cm (⅜–½in) for simple lawn mowing or 2.5–5cm (2–2½in) for a lawn edge trimming machine.

When you have the rough site marked out, drive in a series of level pegs around the area. Get the level of the first peg right by using a datum peg (a peg to which all-over levels may be referred). Then use a spirit level and straight-edge to check all the others. Each peg should be driven in until its top is at the same level as the others (the more pegs you use the more uniform you will be able to make the surface). On average, a fall of about 1 in 100 or so from the house must be incorporated for a patio 3m (10ft) deep. This means that the outermost slabs will be about 3cm (1¼in) lower than those abutting the house wall, so you must adjust your pegs to take this into consideration.

To prepare the site, tamp hardcore (broken stones, bricks and rubble) into the excavated soil.

Fig 29  Standard paving used to create a zigzag edging along an ornamental peat bed of bright heathers.

Hardcore that is carefully tamped will achieve a longer lasting finish, so it might be worth your while hiring a roller or vibrating machine to do the job, especially for a large area. This layer should be 7.5cm (3in) thick. Next comes a 2.5cm (1in) layer of sand which should be raked level and then rolled again and a 2.5cm (1in) layer of mortar in which the slabs can be laid.

Make sure you level the mortar with a screeding board, and then gently compress it. Alternatively, place dots of bedding mortar under the corners and centre of each slab. Lower the slabs into place. Tap each one down lightly, using a piece of wood to cushion the blow and prevent cracking, until there is no tendency for any of them to rock. Use a straight-edge to check that the general paving level is correct before proceeding. Try to plan the paving in such a way that you will not have to cut any of the slabs, as this can be tricky and wasteful. If you are laying crazy paving, you can avoid ragged edges by laying the first slabs at the outer edge and adjoining the house, then working towards the middle.

A joint of about 1.2cm (½in) should be left between the slabs. Keep the joints in line and check continuously with the straight-edge that the slabs are laid uniformly in all planes and that they are flush with each other. An uneven surface is not only dangerous and inconvenient, it is unsightly, and it will tend to collect puddles. Remove the level pegs as you go along and complete the job

Fig 30   Marking out the site.

Fig 31   Digging the site.

Fig 34   Levelling the concrete.

Fig 35   The finished base is ready for laying slabs.

Fig 38   Laying the slabs.

Fig 39   Keeping the slabs even using timber battens.

Fig 32   Levelling the site.

Fig 33   Pouring on the concrete.

Fig 36   Laying the first slab.

Fig 37   Starting the second row of slabs.

Fig 40   The final row of complete slabs.

Fig 41   A slab marked for cutting.

Fig 42   Cutting a slab to fit the shape of patio.

Fig 43   The cut slab.

Fig 44   Fitting the cut slabs.

Fig 45   Shovelling dry cement into the gaps.

Fig 46   Brushing in the dry cement.

Fig 47   Wetting the joints with a watering can.

by pointing the joints either with smoothed mortar infill or just loose sand if you want to grow plants in these joints.

If the patio is on the large size, it may be necessary to make a small rainwater gutter along the lower side, towards a drain or soak-away. It is advisable to keep off the slabs once they are laid for about five days.

## Laying a Continuous Paved Area

Before describing this method, it is worth talking about mixing your own concrete. Concrete has four basic ingredients: cement, clean river sand or sharp sand, aggregate of pebbles and shingle, and water. For a job like this which will be a minimum of three inches thick, the ingredients should be mixed as one part cement, two of sand, and three of aggregate. To find out the volume you need, measure out the area and multiply it by the depth. This gives you your cubic measurement to which you should add a wastage factor of about ten per cent.

If the area to cover is going to be large you should hire a small cement mixer because mixing your own concrete by hand is hard work. The concrete should be mixed until it has an even consistency and colour. It only needs as much water as is necessary to bind the ingredients together into a stiff paste. If the general mix looks like soft mud add more dry ingredients, if it is crumbling add more water. Use a bucket or barrow to measure your proportions accurately. Chemical additives are available for adding to your mix at this stage, to improve the material's frost resistance or to add a coloured finish.

To lay continuous paving you should prepare a good, sound base (see page 35) and observe the same guidelines for drainage. First set in your edge of brick, kerbstone or timber as required, or position a temporary framework of wooden shuttering for a plain concrete finish, making sure that all these borders are level and true. Next, mix and pour on your concrete, in as even a motion as possible, and then smooth the surface roughly with a stout board, such as a scaffold

plank. To achieve a fine concrete finish tamping the board to the edging in a continuous chopping motion. Be careful not to overtamp or the cement mixture will begin to separate, causing weakness in the basic structure. Allow the mixture to harden slightly for about four hours and then render it smooth using a float. This might produce too smooth a surface for your liking so brush with a soft broom (see page 29).

In areas prone to frost, it is a good idea to mix a frost-proofing additive into the concrete (this should be readily available from a builder's merchant). As a final precaution, always cover a newly laid area with a sheet of polythene or tarpaulin if there is any risk of rain or frost before the concrete has completely hardened.

## Building a Split-Level Patio or Terrace

If your house and garden are situated on the bank of a slope, you are going to have to do some levelling in order to make a patio or terrace area. You can turn this to your advantage by designing a split-level patio area or series of terraces. This latter idea is interesting if the land slopes fairly

Fig 48   A raised patio situated away from the house and framed by a fine pergola structure makes the focal point of this garden.

steeply as it will solve any land creep problems. You will have to terrace the slope into a series of levels, hopefully only two although that depends on the height and steepness of the site, each with a retaining wall and connected by steps. All retaining walls must allow for adequate drainage of the remaining soil.

To level the slope the best method to employ is called 'cut and fill'. It involves cutting into the slope, moving the topsoil to the bottom of the garden area (making sure that you do not build great piles of earth, as this will compact the soil and destroy its structure), levelling the subsoil, and replacing the topsoil on the level surface. This leaves you with a flat surface with a bank above it and beneath it.

If the garden area is on a tilt, you can use a similar technique by levelling the site diagonally through the garden. When doing this kind of work, you will have to take into account how close to the house you are digging, as you could

be in danger of weakening its foundations. So with work like this it is best to consult professional landscapers and builders for advice.

Once you have your level areas either in the form of terracing or a split-level patio, the actual laying of a hard surface can continue. But you will have to build a retaining wall against the banks for the reasons described above plus the aesthetic ones which give you the chance to add another dimension to your paved garden areas.

The retaining wall must be designed with the greatest care, for it must be able not only to take the loading of its own mass, but also to withstand all the lateral pressures from the earth. When the soil is waterlogged these pressures can be very great. The best advice is to always allow more wall width than you think you need. In fact, if the wall is much higher than 1.2m (4ft) or on marshy ground, you would be advised to have it designed by a structural engineer. However, with the type of terracing and split-level patio we are

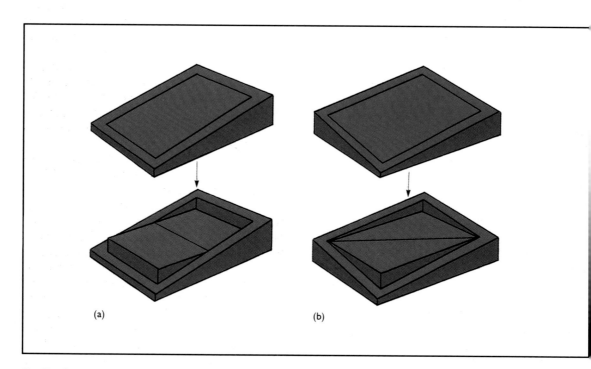

(a)                    (b)

*Fig 49   Cutting and filling to level: (a) a sloping site (b) a tilting site.*

talking about there is no chance of having to build a wall that high.

When designing the retaining wall, look first at structural stability. Loose sandy soils exert the most pressure, as they flow more easily than other types, so make sure it is strong enough at the top and keyed in properly at the base. To help with this, you can slope the wall backwards into the soil which has the effect of working towards the soil's natural angle of repose. Next, look at the appearance of the wall, ideally it should be made of a material that either matches your patio for texture and colour or which complements it. You can use brick, blocks, natural stone and timber. If you use brick or blocks it is best to waterproof the backs to stop efflorescence (this is the development of white salts on the face of bricks). The ground-water salts get carried up into the brickwork and when the water evaporates the salts are left behind on the surface. They can be brushed off but may impair the surface of the brick.

Water drainage is very important as the greatest pressures are exerted when the soil flows easily. So you must provide drainage holes at least every 1–1.5m (3–5ft) near the base of the wall. To encourage the flow of water in these holes, you could lay a strip of gravel behind the hole and then use short lengths of 5cm (2in) diameter downpipe set at a slight incline. For the back wall to the patio area, you would be advised to build a properly formed concrete gulley, passing away to a soak-away and land drains. Otherwise all the water from the bank will run over the paved area and down to the next level – a kind of unintentional water feature. If it is a long, free-standing wall, it will need gaps incorporated in the construction to allow for expansion and contraction.

To construct the wall (which for this purpose is no more than 1m (3ft) high), dig out the soil well into the bank and angle it to discourage it from falling. Form a trench at least 40cm (16in) deep and the same width, incorporating a toe strip about 150mm (6in) deeper at the front. Drive in pegs to establish the level of the concrete (see

page 35). Then lay foundation concrete at least 15–20cm (6–8in) thick. If you think the wall needs reinforcing, insert starter bars – this should not be necessary on a small split-level patio wall.

If the wall is built out of brick, it should be no more than 1m (3ft) high and should be at least 22.5cm (9in) deep, incorporating piers in the front face. Alternatively, you could use the bricks as cladding to mask concrete. Make the concrete 30cm (12in) wide at the base, tapering to about 20cm (8in) at the top. It should also be reinforced with steel rods overlapping the starter bars in the foundations.

Blocks are ideal for using with reinforcing bars. Build the retaining wall with 22.5cm (9in) hollow blocks, use one reinforcing bar, set into well-tamped concrete, every 45cm (18in) of wall length. If you want to construct a stone-retaining wall you will have to find a large number of stones, as it will have to be at least 45cm (18in) thick at the base. It is best to just use facing stones on reinforced concrete. Alternatively, you can build a dry stone-retaining wall which should be reclining back towards the slope, the stones tilting slightly upwards at the front.

To complete the job, you can finish it flush with the higher terrace, or leave a flower border to emphasize the change of level. Alternatively, for safety purposes, you can build a small parapet, about 20–30cm (8–12in) high and surmounted by a low fence.

To get from one level to the other you will also need to construct steps, and these should form an integral and attractive part of your total scheme. Steps should be more than functional, with careful design they can even form the focal point to the whole paved area. The materials used should match or complement the adjacent hard surfacing. Usually, slabs are used for the treads and brick, block or stone for the risers, but all brick, concrete or stone steps can be formed if preferred. The scale of this feature is equally important, as is your choice of material regarding both the structure as a whole and the individual steps. Walking up and down them should be safe and comfortable, so even if only a

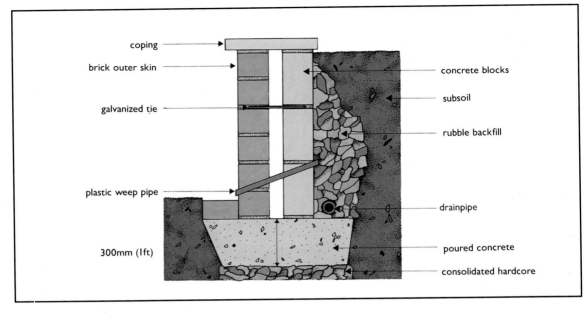

coping

brick outer skin

galvanized tie

plastic weep pipe

300mm (1ft)

concrete blocks

subsoil

rubble backfill

drainpipe

poured concrete

consolidated hardcore

*Fig 50   Low retaining walls must be strongly built and incorporate good drainage.*

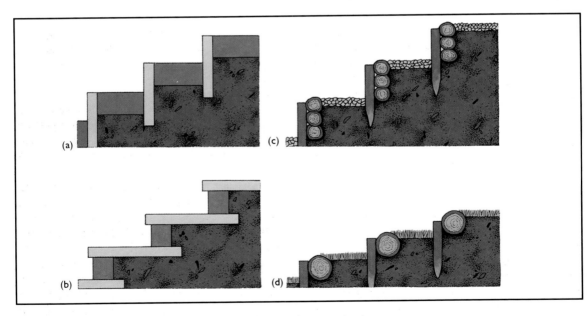

(a)

(b)

(c)

(d)

*Fig 51   Where steps are necessary to link one level to another or to lead from the house or garden, a great many different materials and styles can be used. (a) simple wooden steps using old railway sleepers; (b) paving steps with brick risers; (c) rustic logs held in place with wooden stakes; (d) logs and stakes used to create shallower steps.*

few steps are required, you should allow for plenty of width. Wide steps can look very attractive and if you have the space, give a grand feel to a formal patio or terrace area.

The distance from the front of the step to the back is called the 'going', and it should be about 450mm (18in) in depth but certainly no less than 30cm (12in) as a minimum measurement. The risers should be 10–15cm(4–6in) and never more than 20cm(8in) as a maximum measurement. All this means the whole flight should be between two and three times as long as it is high. The number of steps required can be calculated after measuring the height and angle of the slope. Try to avoid cutting your building materials by working to exact courses of bricks or blocks and slab heights. The steps don't have to follow the slope angle exactly, for variation they can be built out at the bottom or cut into the bank at the top.

Steps have three main components: treads, risers and retaining side walls. The side walls are not strictly speaking necessary, but look good, so if you build them follow the same instructions as for retaining walls.

Begin building with the bottom step by setting a tread into the ground – this is not always needed, but it does improve the scale of the structure, as it really depends on the type of material you are stepping up from. Lay courses of bricks, blocks or stone for the first riser near the back edge of the first tread, and make sure the top line of the riser is level. Clear out some of the soil behind the riser, and if it is soft, lay a compact layer of hardcore blinded with sand. Spread a layer of mortar and bed the next tread in with a 1–1.2cm (⅜–½in) fall to the front. The front of the slab should project 2.5cm (1in) forward of its riser. Continue upwards in a similar manner.

You also might care to build a ramp between the levels, as this is useful for wheelbarrows and other heavy garden appliances or if the garden is used by anyone who is disabled. The slope should be a gradual one, preferably no more than 1 in 10. Most of the materials already discussed are suitable except for gravel, which is too loose. One point to remember is that it is vital for a

Fig 52   Paving can be extended to build matching steps, seating, low walls and raised beds.

good grip to be incorporated into the ramp surface to avoid nasty accidents from slipping.

## Timber Decking

For the average do-it-yourselfer, a ground level deck is the simplest to undertake. Decking raised high off the ground should be built by a skilled professional, as should any decking built on wet or unstable ground.

If the ground is firm and stable, a low-level deck can be installed using metal-fencing support spikes that prevent any part of the wooden supporting posts coming into contact with the ground. These wooden posts should be either 10 × 10cm (4 × 4in) or 15 × 15cm (6 × 6in) depending on the distance being spanned by the bearer timbers, which should be from 7.5 × 10cm (3 × 4in) to 10 × 15cm (4 × 6in). The wood used for the actual walking surface should be 2.5 × 5cm (1 × 2in), 2.5 × 7.5cm (1 × 3in) or even 2.5 × 10cm (1 × 4in), with slightly bevelled edges for a neat finish. You can lay the decking planks either in straight, parallel courses or in attractive zigzag and decorative patterns. However, you must remember that every time the wood changes direction, it will need to be nailed down and this will mean providing supporting timber at these points.

A timber deck adjoining the house, can be supported on one side by a horizontal wall bearer, attached to the house with masonry bolts (expanding rawlbolts). Joists can be extended from the wall bearer to a sturdy support post fixed to a concrete footing at least 60sq cm (24sq in) using a 2.5cm (1in) reinforcing bar as a dowel.

Free-standing decks should not be built more than 1m (3ft) off the ground unless you are an experienced carpenter. Support posts must not be more than 1.8m (6ft) apart and horizontal joists between 1–1.2m (3–4ft) apart. Let the decking timbers overhang the bearers by about 7.5cm (3in) to disguise the supporting structure. Trim the ends of the decking timbers only when the deck is completely finished, to ensure a perfectly straight and neat series of cuts.

All the timbers used in any basic deck construction should be hardwoods which have been initially treated with at least two coats of preservative, after which an annual top-up coat should be sufficient. Softwood can be used for deck surfaces, but it is prone to splintering. For a long-lasting neat finish, use only galvanized nails and screws – brass is expensive but looks the best – and countersink all screw heads to prevent accidents.

You might need a safety rail, especially with raised decks, so use extended support posts to provide the uprights and sturdy coachbolts to attach the horizontal timbers. For the top rail, rounded timber gives a good finish, and it should have a diameter of 75mm (3in). Alternatively, you could use lengths of bamboo or natural and coloured ship's rope as a handgrip.

Decks are ideal to construct on a hillside, because they avoid all that difficult digging out associated with the cut and fill method of levelling ground for terracing. However, they need much stronger supports than low-level decks. There are five main elements to take into account when planning a hillside deck: you must keep the surface light using thin planks; the sub-structure, that is, the joists across the underside of surface boards and main beams, must support 50lb per square foot; there must be posts to support the sub-structure plus concrete piers with a top surface larger than is needed to take post attachments; and finally, there needs to be a concrete footing. This is just to give you an idea of what is involved. Most hillside decks will need professional advice and erection – so cost this out carefully when you are calculating the overall price.

## Roof Gardens

If you have only a flat roof and no ground level garden, it is quite possible to create a delightful garden amongst the chimney pots. And there is no reason why you can't have a patio area as part of it. The only two extra factors that have to be taken into consideration are weight and waterproofing.

The first thing is to check the roof for loading, in order to assess how much weight it can take. Then the waterproofing properties have to be looked at to see if they will be affected, and you must ensure that there is adequate drainage for surplus water to run away correctly through downpipes and so on. To do all this, you will have to liaise with your local authority planning department and it might also be a good idea to seek advice and the services of an architect or structural engineer, before work commences.

A single patio scheme is best for a roof garden but also remember that roofs can be windy places, so some form of screening will be necessary both for you and your plants. But here again keep the screening simple and don't build large stone or brick walls to divide the whole area up, since they will probably be too heavy for the roof anyway. Many conventional paving stones present the same problems, so try and use the lightweight versions that are readily available now or use low-level timber decking as a stylish alternative.

CHAPTER 4

# Protection and Shelter

When planning and building your patio, you should also be looking at some form of shelter or protection from the elements, for both you and the plants. Too much direct sun on a south-facing area will burn everything up and too much wind might drive you indoors on an otherwise perfectly good day. Privacy is also an important factor to consider, as many of us now have backyards rather than palatial gardens, and when you want to relax and unwind either on your own or with the family, you don't necessarily want to see the neighbours.

There are two main groups of protective structures; overhead, like pergolas and arches, and side-screening types, like walls, trellises and hedges. With careful planning and siting these structures should enhance the patio as well as serve an essentially useful purpose. Many styles look good in their own right but will also provide good support for climbing plants and allow you to experiment with vertical planting ideas. Thus protective structures will give you the chance to turn the whole patio area into a fascinating combination of shapes and colours, once it is finished.

However, you must first plan your structures. For each type, there are a whole array of different designs and materials at varying costs, so your final choice will be determined both by style and budget. There are few ground rules and it really is a matter of personal preference and common sense. For example, a smart modern patio block wall would look somewhat out of place on a country-style patio adjoining an old cottage. Equally, a rustic trellis might look odd and rather dilapidated screening a sleek city backyard with its geometric pavers and predominance of brick.

## WALLS

If you are thinking of building a wall for shelter and privacy, it is more likely than not to be a free-standing type rather than a retaining wall, so at this stage it is better to concentrate on how to build these. They are usually made of brick, concrete or stone. There is a splendidly wide choice

Fig 53 Ornamental columns and a low wall produce the effect of viewing the rest of the garden through open windows.

45

*Fig 54    The trellis is equally useful for decorating blank walls and providing a support for climbing plants.*

of bricks to choose from (*see* page 29) and even different types of mortar which can alter the appearance of the finished wall. Depending on how well the mortar and brick blend in colour and style, you can either have the grout indented or, if they are well co-ordinated, leave it flush. Your chosen method of laying the bricks will also affect its look and strength (*see* page 100). The most common way is to lay the bricks side-on and then finish off with the bricks end-on at the top of the wall. However, you can use the end-on technique for any of the courses (rows) throughout the structure, to create patterns and designs by mixing them with side-on bricks, provided that the wall structure maintains bond stability. To give the structure bond stability, you must ensure that each layer overlaps properly with the gap between each brick parallel with the centre of the brick above and below (*see* page 98).

Choice of material is very important, as it dic-

tates not only the look, but also what you can do with the wall when it is finished. You have to decide whether it is to be left bare, painted or covered in plants. If you add paint the texture of the material you use has to be considered more closely. For instance, concrete no longer has to be plain and special patio walling blocks come with all sorts of different rough or lined finishes. If you are leaving the wall bare, it will become something of a focal point, so the choice of material is clearly very important and ought to be something fairly decorative such as brick or stone. Covering it with plants may mean it does not matter what you use, but it must be strong enough to take the weight. If you plan to grow twining plants, or any species that needs training and does not cling naturally to a rough surface, you will need some sort of metal eye for them to cling to. These eyes should be fixed at the construction stage.

Another point to remember before you start building is that free-standing walls differ from house walls in that both sides are open to the elements. So select materials that are known to be frost resistant.

The foundations of the wall should be twice as thick as the wall itself and made of concrete mixed in general as two parts sand, six parts gravel and one part cement. This is then poured between wood frames on to a firm subsoil below the frost line. If the wall is going to be particularly high, sink vertically positioned steel rods into the concrete foundation for reinforcement. If the wall is going to be brick, either thread the rods through holed bricks and mortar round them or build a pier when using solid bricks, remembering to cement the rods inside the pier.

The thickness of the wall depends on the height, but as a guide brick walls over 60cm (2ft) should be two to three bricks thick. Walls made out of pre-cast concrete blocks up to 1.2m (4ft) high can be one block thick. The mortar prepared when building a brick wall should always be less strong than the brick, so that when any water present in the brick freezes causing it to expand, the give will be in the mortar and not the bricks.

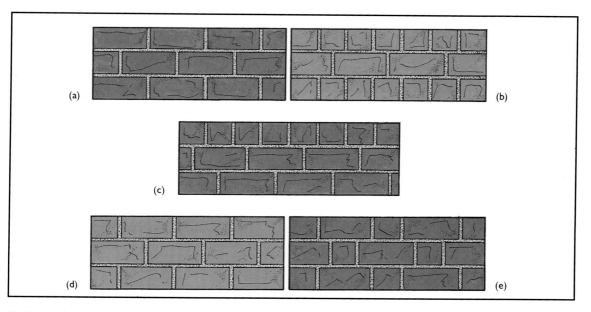

Fig 55 Bricks can be laid in a variety of ways influencing both strength and appearance: (a) stretcher bond – bricks laid lengthways, good for single leaf walls; (b) English bond – alternate courses of stretchers and headers; (c) English garden wall bond – two or more courses of stretchers to one of headers; (d) Flemish wall bond – one header and three stretchers on each course; (e) Flemish bond – alternate stretchers and headers on each course.

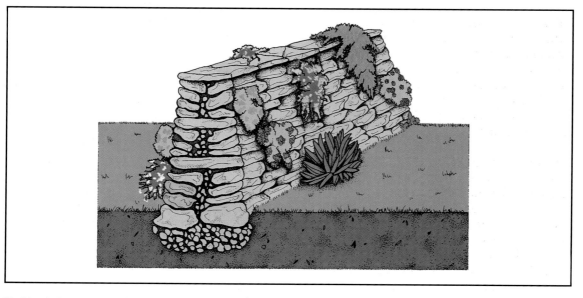

Fig 56 A dry stone wall is perfect for an informal, natural look and can be interplanted with colourful trailing and smothering plants.

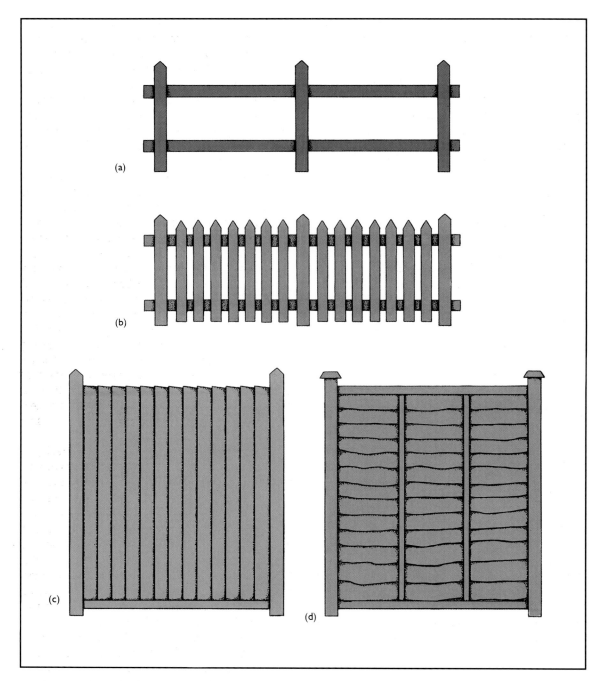

*Fig 57   There are many types of fencing to choose from, depending on how much privacy and protection you require: (a) simple post and rail; (b) picket fence; (c) feather-edged boards; (d) lapped timber panels for maximum privacy.*

If you are planning a long run of wall, further stability can be given by building buttresses at regular intervals along the length. Long runs will also need expansion joints to take up any movement that occurs when the wall heats up and cools with normal temperature changes. These expansion joints are vertical gaps which break the solid barrier. It is a good idea to make these joints wider than is strictly necessary, say 22.5cm (9in) so you can use them as a kind of window.

Depending on where you live, the local availability of stone and the style of garden you are planning, dry stone walls are a very attractive if informal option. A well-built free-standing dry stone wall is very stable and its interesting variety of textures and effects can look superb in the right surroundings. The wall should be laid on a base of sand, hardcore or concrete foundations and the width of the base must be equal to half its height. If it is correctly built, the wall should taper from base to cap. Set it upon two large stones and build on these so that each stone leans slightly downwards and the whole structure inwards. Infill the middle with smaller stones. These types of wall are excellent for covering with plants and give you all kinds of different planting possibilities.

# FENCES

A cheaper and more easily erected protection for the patio than a wall is a fence. Here again, the choice of styles is extensive. Presumably you don't want a basic boundary fence around a patio area as these are not particularly attractive to look at, so take the trouble to check out some of the alternatives which are a bit more expensive but well worth it for setting off a well planned patio area. For example, you could use woven or lapped wood panels. Unless specially treated against rot, these panels are not that long lasting, but they can be replaced singly as it becomes necessary, providing you with the opportunity to tidy up the fence as a whole at the same time. Another alternative is ranch-style

fencing, which is strong, long lasting and fairly easy to erect. However, this more open style cannot be used as a wind-break and if you need your fence to provide privacy, then dense climbers or twiners will have to be grown over it. For this type of fence, the post should be about 100mm (4in) square and the rails should be 15 × 2cm (6in × ¾in) and simply nailed to the posts once the post tops are level. The nailing should be inclined to give added strength.

The most decorative form of fencing and probably the best for a good looking patio is the type based round a form of trellis panel. Basically each panel is made of laths set at intervals to create a framework, of which 10cm (4in) is considered to be the ideal. The posts should be about 7.5cm (3in) square and the main framework to take the panel should measure 5 × 3.5cm (2 × 1½in) and be nailed into the posts. Battens are used on each side. One side is nailed in first and then locked in the framework by nailing the other. You can give the posts a more stylish finish by putting on decorative caps, and these can be rounded or chamfered. If you aren't prepared to construct this type of boundary screening yourself, there is a whole range of different designs of trellis panels readily available from garden centres and specialist manufacturers.

Before erecting a fence or length of trellis, all wooden structures should be treated for rot and insect attack. Fence posts can rot below the surface too, so particular care should be taken to treat these parts. It is possible to overcome this by fixing a metal anchor to the base of the wooden post and then sinking the metal into a concrete foundation. For wooden posts, the foundations do not have to be concrete, though this provides greater stability. If you set the posts directly into the soil, place a large stone at the bottom of the hole to help drainage.

The first step for the actual construction is to stake out the line of fence and run a string between the stakes. Next, mark the position of the fence posts. Some people are tempted to use a handy tree in the line as a fence post, but remember that trees change as they grow and eventually they could ruin the line and look of your fence. You are better off allowing some breathing room and growing space between your fence and the tree.

Panel fences are one of the best types for patios, being inexpensive and easy to erect. Once the first post is firm and plumb, you should stretch a taut piece of string between the top of it and a stake set in at the far end of the fence. The string is to indicate the exact height of the panel tops. You should rest the panel on bricks or timber to keep it about 5cm (2in) clear of the ground as this will prevent rotting. Then butt it up to the centre of the side of the first post. At-tach the panel on both sides with galvanized nails. Now set the second post in its hole, bring-ing it into firm contact with the other edge of the panel. Check that both post and panel are plumb and level, then ram earth and hardcore into the hole. You then proceed in this way, ensuring that the panel tops are accurately located along the guide line. If you have a patio on two levels it will be necessary to step the panels. Remember in this case that you will need one post whose length is greater by the amount of the step.

## HEDGES

Although they take far longer to establish themselves, hedges make an excellent natural wind-break and offer protection from all weathers, with the added attraction of changing shape and colour through the seasons. You can plan to have flowering hedges to add seasonal colour, evergreens for year-round interest and protection, or a variety with good autumn colour.

The main disadvantage of hedges is that they do take a long time to grow to maturity, so some temporary means of screening will also be necessary until it has grown a little. A hedge also needs greater maintenance because it requires regular feeding, clipping and general tidying.

However, even these drawbacks can be over-come by choosing the right species. For instance, you might need a quick grower for your new

Fig 58 A peephole window cut in a well-grown and well-maintained hedge.

patio to provide privacy. In this case, you might consider the evergreen and golden-flowered Berberis x stenophylla which will grow to around six feet after six years, or be attracted by the pinkish flowers of Escallonia macrantha which will grow to around eight foot in six years in a moderate climate. A good deciduous species is Japonica Chaenomeles speciosa which has crim-son flowers and will grow to about 2m (6ft) in five years.

If you don't mind waiting and you want a hedge that will ultimately be easy to maintain, you should be looking at slow-growing evergreens like Chamaecyparis lawsoniana 'Green Hedger' or Thuja plicata 'Atrovirens'. The latter is a Western red cedar that should grow both bushy and upright. Plant these species about two foot apart and trim in the late summer, using secateurs on

Fig 59   Here a turf bank produces an almost instant hedging effect that simply needs watering and cutting with shears.

the *Thuja* to keep it bushy. Common yew, beech and hornbeam are also worth considering as hedging material since they won't require much maintenance, yet can take clipping into shape.

If you are planning to plant a hedge the best time to prepare the ground is in autumn or winter, when you should mark out a 4ft wide strip along the length of the new hedge. Dig a trench one spade blade deep along one side of the strip and move the soil beyond the other side. It is useful to remove all the weeds you find at this stage. Next, spread compost in the bottom of the trench and then dig a second trench, turning the soil straight into the first one. Continue this digging, weeding and composting process until you reach the far end of the strip when you should fill this last trench with the soil you took from the first. The site should then be left for about two weeks to allow the soil to settle. If you want, you can scatter in an appropriate fertilizer and then hoe it. After two weeks you can put in your hedging plants. The

spacing between them is usually about 45–60cm (18in–2ft), but it is best to check first with your garden centre or supplier. Hedging plants are frequently planted too close together which is fair enough if you want the hedge to thicken quickly and you are prepared to thin out before overcrowding starts to affect general growth.

## SCREENS AND TRELLISES

A screen can be a very adaptable form of windbreak, especially if you have a portable type that you can move around the patio area, either to help shade you from the sun or to cut out a cool breeze. You could make these yourself, making sure you used materials that looked right outdoors, simply by stapling paper, fabric, hessian or other woven material to a wooden frame. More permanent screens available include bamboo screens – the perfect natural backdrop to bamboos and other leafy plants, willow hurdles

51

*Fig 60 Screens are often highly decorative apart from serving a practical purpose: (a) timber louvres look light yet still maintain privacy; (b) laying panels of louvres in different directions to create patterns; (c) simple wooden frames infilled with bamboo, wattle, rush or other lightweight screening panels; (d) canvas screening can be useful for temporary or seasonal protection or shading.*

and woven reeds and grasses. These screens, whether fixed or portable, are made in a similar way to trellis fencing. You have to affix your chosen material inside the wooden frame, then either permanently attach it to say the post of an archway or the side of your house, or construct some form of free-standing footing for it. Make sure if you do want a portable screen, that it is not too heavy to move around.

The most basic form of garden trellis is not really substantial enough to act as a major boundary structure, but it is ideal for fixing to walls, or maybe to attach to a wooden post to break up a large area. Once it is smothered in climbing plants, it will certainly provide privacy, though it may not be substantial enough to withstand strong winds. However, if you want to hide a large obtrusive wall or other unsightly construction near your patio, a simple criss-cross series of

galvanized steel wires spaced regularly over the wall surface is a good way to make a cheap trellis. Drill and plug holes in the appropriate positions in the mortar and use stainless steel, galvanized or black painted screws to avoid rust marks on the wall. Alternatively, you can use a wooden trellis or plastic mesh. Both types need to be fixed so that there is a gap between the wall and the trellis. If you want to hide something like a water butt, small pieces of wooden trellis can be built all round it and fixed to a nearby post or wall. The butt will have to be in a fairly sheltered place though to prevent wind damage.

A more permanent trellis is the good old rustic-style one which you can make up in patterns as simple or complicated as you like. The construction of these is the same as for pergolas (see pages 54–6) and uses simple poles in chestnut or a similar rot-proof timber nailed together in

*Fig 61  A staggered trellis makes an attractive screen without blocking out all the light.*

Fig 62   *This ornamental trellis creates a formal effect and keeps the patio completely private.*

squared or diagonal framework designs. For something a little more sophisticated, there are more decorative (and expensive) trellises in stained or painted timber. These might vary from the simplest, most basic grid design to sturdy structures complete with sweeping profiles, finials and other decorations based on traditional designs such as Victorian Gothic and medieval.

## PERGOLAS

A pergola can transform an area of your patio or a path leading to it into an interesting open tunnel, covered in fragrant and colourful climbing plants. It is important that the structure is not too narrow so that its use and access is restricted. Its basic construction is a series of three members; the uprights, cross rails and side members.

The uprights should be spaced no more than 2.4m (8ft) apart and should not be less than 10cm (4in) in diameter. You can do all sorts of creative things with the crossrails providing they are a minimum of 7.5cm (3in) in diameter or square. You could, if you like the idea, use wider but thinner crossrails such as planking. This produces a sturdier look. To give climbing plants a helping hand you could attach a series of longitudinal laths about 5 × 2.5cm (2 × 1in). It is also a good idea to fix wires along the top members for the same purpose.

You can also construct pergola supports out of brick or stone but because the effect is quite dominant, you really need a good-sized garden or patio to carry the effect off successfully. This technique also works out to be much more expensive. The most popular style of pergola is the rustic type which is easy to erect using simple poles. Larch or chestnut poles are the best timber to use and you can leave the bark on if

Fig 63   Pergolas can be constructed in whatever materials suit the style and scale of your patio; this simple arrangement of larch poles creates an unmistakeably rustic appearance.

felled in winter, otherwise it will begin to peel off. However, it may be that this informal look suits your particular scheme.

The upright posts are sunk into the ground after being well treated with preservative. The depth should be about 60cm (2ft) if possible as this aids a longer life. They should be wedged in with rubble and loosely covered with earth. You can use a cement or concrete filling but then the posts tend to rot at ground level.

Saw the top rails to be fitted to the posts before nailing them home. Similarly, the uprights can be sawn in advance to take the lower rails. The timbers over the top will be firmer for having notches cut to slot on top of the upper rails. The additional lower rails to help climbing plants should be sawn to the appropriate angle if you have them in the traditional V shape. The nails in the V-shaped uprights should go into the main poles and the lower rail at an angle,

whereas the top timbers should be nailed vertically into the cross-pieces.

If you think a pergola is too much for your terrace or patio, then an archway which leads into the garden would be a good idea for adding height and weight to your scheme. If you want a simple arch, it can be constructed in the same way as the pergola, except that it is narrower and slimmer. A typical rustic arch can be formed with basic frames consisting of a pair of uprights topped with a head-piece using 7.5cm (3in) poles, and with two 5cm (2in) internal braces under the head. The frames are then linked with 5cm (2in) struts and braces.

If you want a more complicated arch, you could plan building one into your brick or stone wall; however, this may depend on how good a builder you are. You must remember that at the very least you'll need a wooden template for your design. Unless you are very competent and

Fig 65  *Bamboo or rush mats can be rolled out over a pergola to shade an eating or seating area at the hottest times of the day.*

already experienced in this kind of construction work it might be best to leave this sort of arch to a professional builder.

## GAZEBOS

You might consider covering the whole of your patio area in an open framework so that plants can climb right over giving a sheltered, shady feel with only dappled sunlight getting through. By doing this you will be creating a kind of gazebo, although strictly speaking this should be on a mound overlooking a fine garden view or positioned in the centre of the lawn.

You can still buy classic metal gazebos, either original antiques or reproduction styles, but these are very expensive and may not be the

Fig 64 (Opposite)  *An ornamental gazebo contributes shade and is a highly decorative feature.*

right size and shape to fit your patio plans. A simple wooden structure would look equally good in most gardens and is easy enough to construct and install. You need six main posts separated by equal distances and three cross-pieces to make the open roof structure. The size of these cross-pieces depends on the size of gazebo you want. So again, it is best to make a scale drawing so you know exactly what you want before starting on the work. This type of structure looks best with a low wall built round it, with a gateway for access. So do remember that if you plan this, the upright posts should be sunk before the wall is built, otherwise you will be making life more difficult for yourself.

Finishing the roof off may depend on what type of plants you wish to grow. You might want to add a netting over the top and even build trellising on the uprights. If you use netting, the best type is the prefabricated green netting, that is readily available from garden centres.

57

**CHAPTER 5**

# Planting Ideas and Containers

The patio or terrace is not only a special area for sitting outside and relaxing, it is also an ideal place for growing plants. Indeed, it would certainly look strangely bare and rather barren without them. You should allow lots of room for plants in your patio scheme, maybe incorporating bordering beds and island beds within the main area of the patio. You can also leave cracks between the paving so that creeping plants can spread, giving the whole area a much softer feel and breaking up the formal lines of hard paving. Walls should not be left bare. You can attach some form of trellis or support wires and grow climbers and twiners up them, creating a kind of living curtain for your outside room.

Containers are especially useful for patios, as they enable plants to be displayed on paved surfaces and play a vital role in your patio design. The plants you choose to fill them with, and how you choose to position them, either singly or in groups, will drastically alter the appearance of the finished area. And, since they are so flexible, these are features that can change with the seasons or with your own tastes by replanting. The containers themselves may be moved around to redesign the area at any time.

Containers are useful to break up areas of unrelenting paving by adding curves, new shapes, textures and a little height, to create an environment far more restful on the eyes. You could place a number of matching containers in a sweep round a corner of the patio or position one big container in a corner and surround it with large pebbles for added interest and again

to round off an empty square shape. Steps can be made more of a feature by placing a container on each tread where it abuts the side wall. Large pots planted with a small tree, shrub or formal topiary subject can be positioned either side at the start of a flight or beside an arch or doorway.

Trough-type planters attached to walls and window-boxes (if a house window overlooks the area) add new shapes and help break up vertical surfaces. Hanging baskets, either suspended from brackets fixed to the wall or attached to overhead constructions like pergolas and free-standing poles, are also useful for creating an all-round feeling of lush green foliage and colour. There are many different types of container to choose from (see pages 59–70).

More permanent planting features like raised

*Fig 66 Stone or wooden troughs can be planted with a variety of plants to produce a good blend of shapes and colours.*

beds can also mask the hard lines of brick or paving, and make the patio scheme altogether more interesting, especially if they are carefully planted with the right types of plants. They can also help give the area a more lived-in and mature look very quickly.

Water features should also be considered as a means of displaying some striking and beautiful plants, offering you a whole new planting group to experiment with. Such features could be as simple as an old sink or lined wooden barrel, up to the more complicated and specially constructed formal and informal pools (see pages 73–8). Remember, though, to try and keep these features to an appropriate scale within the size of the total patio area.

## CONTAINERS

### Clay Pots

The traditional terracotta clay pot is warm and pleasing to the eye and is available in a wide range of sizes from about 50mm (2in) in diameter up to 30–35.5cm (12–14in). There are also giant ones for larger plants with diameters of 45–61cm (18–24in) that can look really stunning in the right setting, with or without plants. Styles range widely from the traditional plain pots to fancy or decorated types, in the style of Venetian, Tuscan or Minoan earthenware. These latter pots are usually in the larger sizes and designed for display, as well as being often available in different shades

Fig 67  An arrangement of matching clay containers on different levels.

*Fig 68  Small pots and containers grouped together to make a leafy arrangement at the foot of a narrow flight of steps.*

and colours. You can also buy glazed terracotta pots which look rather more sophisticated, but which are not porous. These might be used for display only or as cache-pots – an ornamental container in which plant and pot are slipped. Clay pans, about one third of the height of the pots, are often used for growing alpines and seeds, and you can also buy half-pots (which are about half the size of normal pots) and these are ideal for low-growing plants.

Clay pots are naturally complementary to all kinds of plants and the smaller sizes are the best for propagating plants. When looking for pots purely for display purposes you should not use any smaller than 15cm (6in) in diameter on the patio, since containers below this size tend to dry out too quickly. Pots 15cm (6in) and above are recommended for all permanent plants, including shrubs, trees, fruit bushes and large perennials.

Clay containers are porous; this accelerates the compost's moisture loss and creates the danger of plants drying out too quickly in hot weather. Conscientious watering and mulching any exposed areas of soil with peat, pebbles or wood chips is the best remedy. Porosity can work to your advantage, however, because when the pots are stood in matching saucers of water they will absorb the moisture, and the saucers will prevent any discolouration or staining of your paving surface. Clay pots are particularly suitable for plants such as herbs, which need a well-drained soil, and due to their weight, they are also good stable companions for large or heavy plants. Unfortunately, they are easily chipped or broken, and can be damaged by frost (even some of the so-called frost-resistant types, if the frost is very severe). They will often develop a mossy growth on the outside, giving a soft green bloom which most owners leave uncleaned

*Fig 69   Weathered terracotta gives an immediately mellow effect to your scheme.*

to give a mellow, aged appearance. This aged appearance is perfect for country-style or informal patios.

## Plastic Pots

These are available in a similar range of sizes to clay pots, including half-pots and pans. However, they are much cheaper than clay pots, especially the large sizes, but if you use these on the patio, they benefit from being inserted inside another, more ornamental container as they are not very attractive. They do come in traditional terracotta colour and black which do not look too bad within a well-planned scheme. However, try to avoid the white and green types which tend to stand out rather than blend with other patio features.

Plastic pots could be a good choice for plants that like moist conditions, as the compost does not dry out so rapidly, but they are not such an ideal choice for plants, such as alpines and bulbs, which need good drainage. The compost can remain wet for a long time, especially if you are heavy-handed with the watering, which can be worse than letting the plant dry out. After a number of years the plastic can also become brittle, and is easily cracked or broken. A further disadvantage is that the combination of a plastic pot and a soilless compost results in a very light container, so large plants may be blown over, even in the lightest of winds.

## Window-Boxes and Wall-Troughs

If your patio has any boundary walls and especially if a house window overlooks the area, window-boxes and wall-troughs are ideal for breaking up the monotony of a blank vertical area. Looking at window-boxes first, you will find types bought from a garden centre will be made of traditional wood, plastic and (heavy and expensive, but most attractive), terracotta clay. If you are a reasonable carpenter, you can make your own easily enough. Home-made boxes can cost next to nothing, they have perpendicular sides and can be designed to fit the exact length and width of a window-sill using second-hand floor boards. The ideal height is 12.5–15cm (5–6in), although you can vary this by cutting single boards along their length or by adding two boards side by side.

Due to the weight of the soil, home-made window-boxes often end up bulging. However, this can be overcome by reinforcing the side joints. Cut a slot in the edge of one piece, 5cm (2in) long, and to the width of the shank of a galvanised screw with a hole at one end, of the same diameter as the head of the screw. On the edge of the adjoining piece, drive in the screw with its head protruding to the depth of the slot. Insert the head of the screw in the hole of the first plank and hammer the end of the second plank in the direction of the groove. The sharp edge of the screw will cut its way through the first plank. Finally, saw the ends square.

To keep the box upright and take into consideration the slope of the window-sill, stand a spirit-level across the sill. When the bubble comes to rest in the centre, measure the distance to the edge of the sill and make the front of the box that much higher. Bore a number of holes in the bottom of the box and cut slots in the bottom of the front piece to allow water to drain away. The water drips should be taken away by the drip channel under the sill, making sure the wall below does not get wet.

When the box is finished, treat it inside and out with a clear horticultural wood preservative (one that will not kill plants). You will also need brackets to help hold it in place, black wrought iron being the most attractive.

When building your own window-box, make sure the grain runs vertically in the end pieces to provide a firm grip for the screws. This leaves the end grain at the top exposed to soak up water,

so cover it with aluminium or zinc tape or you can pin on half-round wood mouldings or strip-wood at each corner.

For extra long sills, a central reinforcement the same size as the end pieces might be needed in the box, thus dividing it into two compartments. If you purchase a window-box from a garden centre, the slope of the sill will not have been taken into account so you will have to provide wedges under the front edge of the box to keep it straight.

A wall-trough can be made in exactly the same way as a window-box, although you will have to support it on good brackets, making sure they are strong enough to take the combined weight of container, soil and plants. To lessen the load on your brackets you could consider placing the trough on the top of a wall that has been built for shelter or screening. A whole series of troughs could be placed along the top of a wall in this way, and they could all be held in place with light-weight brackets. Alternatively, you could build brick troughs as the finish to the wall top and just fill them with soil, making sure they were lined to avoid water soaking through and efflorescence appearing on the brick face. Whichever method you choose, it is important to drain the trough and you must make holes in the same way for window-boxes. Here though, there will be no sill drip channel and the dirty water would run down the wall, staining and dampening it. This can be overcome by giving the wall underneath the trough an application of silicone waterproofing liquid which is colourless and repels water.

## Free-Standing Troughs

These are usually long rectangular plant containers of a good depth. There are many designs, including classical imitations, to choose from, and they may be made from timber, concrete or fibreglass. You can also get old stone or lead troughs and tanks which are greatly sought after – try architectural salvage yards for these – although it is now possible to buy new and reconstituted stone troughs.

Fig 70  *A series of small troughs make a feature of these outside stairs.*

Stone and concrete troughs are best raised off the ground on bricks or blocks of wood to ensure good drainage, but wood or fibreglass types can be supported on their own set of matching legs, usually organized in a basic trestle arrangement.

## Low, Flat Bowls

Low, flat, concrete bowls have become popular over the last forty years and they can look very effective as part of a modern scheme, particularly when planted with brightly coloured summer bedding plants. These should be cleared in the autumn and then bulbs planted for early spring colour. The bulbs should then be removed when they are finished, to be replaced with annual summer bedding plants again to maintain a

Fig 71  *A large shallow container makes the ideal centre-piece for a formal patio.*

Fig 72   Look out for different sizes and shapes of container that can be
used to display various types of plants in massed groups.

continuous display, in what are rather plain but
functional containers.

## Urns and Jars

Urns and jars often have fairly narrow necks,
which can be a disadvantage, since few plants
look in proportion to the container. However,
they are still marvellous unplanted for adding
height and elegance to a co-ordinated pot arrangement, the total group creating a focal point
on the patio and helping create a sun-drenched
atmosphere.

Urns are often shaped like the funerary urns of
the ancient Greeks and Romans, and have been
popular for garden decoration since the seven-
teenth century. For a different effect, try raising
them above eye-level, on piers or a wall for example, as an ornamental focal point. Where they
do permit planting up, urns and jars look at their
best on the classic terrace planted with a tall

elegant plant in the middle, surrounded by
softening trailers.

If you are looking for large, deep containers for
your plants – this is important for trees, shrubs
and perennials that need plenty of space for
roots – you will find a wide range of broad tubs,
planters and barrels in a choice of materials,
readily available at most garden centres. These
can be very decorative and are suitable for both
permanent planting arrangements and seasonal
bedding displays. Designs can be chosen to suit
formal modern settings as well as the smartly laid
out terraces of period town-houses and the
country cottage-style courtyard.

## Tubs

Tubs are basically large, deep containers that can
be used for larger permanent plants such as
shrubs, trees and climbers. They are also useful
for displaying massed arrangements of spring and

Fig 73   A classically-styled urn filled with foliage plants.

Fig 74   This smart but small town patio offers both privacy and a wide range of features in the minimum of space.

summer bedding plants. Tubs are available in various materials, but wood is the best choice for a hot, sunny position, as the soil moisture takes longer to evaporate causing the compost to dry out less rapidly.

Tubs can be bought as cut-down barrels from garden centres; however, they will need to be treated with a horticultural timber preservative and have holes drilled in the base for drainage, before being used. Purpose-made ornamental timber tubs are also available, sometimes called Versailles tubs and they may be round or square-shaped, often with decorative finials on all four corners. The square ones look good planted with a tree (especially an ornamentally clipped bay or citrus tree) or large shrub, and traditionally had removable side panels to allow for easy extraction of the plant when it needed a fresh supply of compost or potting on to a larger tub. Although the traditional style of wooden tub is still available, you will be lucky to find one with removable sides these days. So if you want this facility then you'll have to construct your own.

Wooden tubs can be naturally stained or painted. However, they are usually plain white, as bright colours don't tend to look right against plants and other patio features, although some styles of patio can be complemented by pretty pastel shades. If you do want to paint your tubs, bear in mind the type and colour range of the plants they will be holding, and the backdrop against which they will be positioned – red brick, grainy timber or white concrete. A subtle contrast is always more effective than too close a shade which causes the container to fade into the background.

Concrete containers are readily available, are relatively inexpensive and come in a large selection of shapes and sizes, including the largest and tallest geometric planter shapes which are suitable for a large collection of plants in a modern setting. A more traditional and informal setting would be better complemented by real or imitation stone tubs, copying old-fashioned designs which are sometimes highly ornamented. Tub sizes vary a great deal but the most useful ones are 50cm (20in) in diameter and 40cm (16in) high and 40cm (16in) in diameter and 35.5cm (14in) high.

As with troughs, it is best to stand tubs on blocks of brick or wood, raising them off the ground slightly to ensure better drainage of any surplus water. Should you be planting a collection of species that prefers a damp soil, matching saucers or trays beneath is a better option.

## Planters

These are very large containers intended for groups of plants such as shrubs and perennials, almost like free-standing raised flower-beds. They can be used for bedding and bulbs as well,

Fig 75  Unusual timber containers for climbing plants are useful for adding height to your scheme.

but their great advantage over tubs and smaller containers is that they give you greater scope for a variety of more permanent planting schemes. The planter is a portable container (although you are unlikely to want to move it far once it is in position, filled with soil and plants) and is either square or rectangular, being made out of timber, fibreglass or plastic. You can make your own wooden planter out of timber planks 2.5cm (1in) thick assembled into a simple box shape. For special tips and hints on construction (*see* page 62).

A good depth for any planter is 45–60cm (18–24in). This will allow plants plenty of deep

*Fig 76 Petunias can be relied on for a brilliant summer display, especially when planted en masse in a large container.*

root space and the compost will not dry out so rapidly in hot weather. Planters are very useful in basement patio areas and on existing paved areas where you will not have the opportunity to create *in situ* beds. They look good on all styles of patio where you haven't set aside any areas for natural beds.

As with tubs, planters ideally should be raised a few inches off the ground for added drainage. Also, if the planter is in close contact with the ground, a seal consisting of soil particles and algae is likely to form around the bottom edges which will impede drainage and cause possible fungal problems.

## Barrels

Full-sized barrels can be used for all kinds of plants, but are mainly used with planting holes inserted in the sides. These can be planted with herbs or strawberry plants, and it is possible to cover the whole area on the outside with greenery and coloured fruits or flowers to great effect. Large barrels used without planting holes on the outside, can make plants in the top look rather out of proportion in relation to the height of the container. If you do use a barrel in this way, the best choice of plants would be trailing species so the bare sides are covered as much as possible.

## Growing Bags

If your garden is very small and the patio area has taken up most of it, or if you just have a paved backyard or city basement area, then growing bags are an ideal short-term container for growing your own vegetables.

Growing bags are long, narrow polythene bags filled with soilless compost that is available from a variety of different manufacturers (you'll see plenty on display at your local garden centre). The average length is 1.2m (4ft), but smaller ones are available. In most new types, the compost comes in the form of a dehydrated compressed slab easily transportable. Once the bag is set in place, water is added and the slab swells up to fill the bag with compost. Most growing bags are not very attractive though, coming in glaring plastic colours and with the manufacturer's name emblazoned on them. It is possible to get plain brown or stone-coloured bags to match the patio surface, so look out for these, unless you are prepared to disguise the growing bag completely, by surrounding it with a line of bricks and covering the surface of the bag with aggregate.

It is possible to get extremely good growth from the specially prepared compost, provided the plants are fed regularly once they have established themselves. The bags do not dry out as quickly as pots, so be careful with the watering. They must be placed on a firm, level surface, then following the manufacturer's instructions, a hole is cut in the top for each individual plant. Apart from this, there is no special planting technique. However, as the compost is soilless, you should remember to firm it in very lightly when planting, in order to prevent compressing the compost. A 1.2m (4ft) bag will comfortably hold three to four tomato or pepper plants, or two melon or cucumber plants.

Most manufacturer's recommend that you do not make holes in the bottom of the bag for drainage, so again, do be careful not to overwater as this will saturate the compost. If the manufacturer of your bags does recommend drainage holes in the base (these will be marked on the bag), you can prevent problems from drips and stains on the patio surface by standing them on shallow trays containing gravel.

Tall crops such as tomatoes will need supporting, so use proprietary growing bag crop supports. These are usually made from plastic-coated steel, and have special feet which are placed under the bag so the weight of the bag then supports the frame. You can't use normal bamboo canes for support as there is insufficient depth of compost to hold them. Another way to support the tall plants is to place the bag against a wall and tie the plants to a trellis or horizontal wires fixed to the wall. As they grow, the plants will soon use up the fertilizer in the compost so it is important to feed them regularly – about once a week. Liquid fertilizer is the easiest feed to use, but make sure the compost is moist before adding it.

## Strawberry Barrels

This is the name given to those barrels with holes in the side (see page 68). They are not difficult to make, and can be constructed easily from re-cycled barrels by obtaining a used full-sized barrel and drilling 5cm (2in) diameter holes in the side about 20cm (8in) apart, staggering them across the face of the barrel. Alternatively, you can buy proprietary white PVC or natural terracotta strawberry tubs direct from garden centres. These tubs have the roots of the plants pushed through the holes as they are filled with compost, and finish up with about four plants in their top.

## Hanging Baskets

Hanging baskets are ideal to give overhead colour to the patio area and liven up any overhead structure like a pergola or gazebo. The traditional basket is made from galvanized wire, but more modern types are made from plastic-coated wire. Both these types hang from chains. Another type is the solid plastic basket, built with a drip tray that hangs from a chain or plastic hanger. The colours of these types include green, white, black and terracotta. Some versions even have built-in water reservoirs. Large baskets have

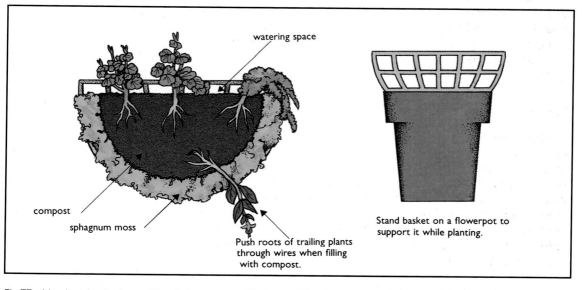

watering space

compost

sphagnum moss

Push roots of trailing plants through wires when filling with compost.

Stand basket on a flowerpot to support it while planting.

Fig 77 Line hanging baskets with sphagnum moss, fill them with compost and push the roots of trailing plants through the wires. Standing the basket on a bucket or large pot will help keep it stable while planting.

Fig 78 Old stone sinks and millwheels make excellent containers for alpines and other low-growing patio plants.

a diameter of 30–45cm (12–18in), small ones measure about 20cm (8in). Depth can vary from 15–23cm (6–9in). Wall-mounted baskets are also available and look good on bare brick or stone walls and again may be solid plastic or wire. You can also obtain a wide variety of hanging pots in either plastic or terracotta.

Baskets have to be lined with sphagnum moss, proprietary liners or polythene sheeting with drainage holes before filling. The full baskets should be checked daily for water requirements as they will dry out rapidly in hot weather. They should also be fed regularly once the plants are established – about once a week.

## Sink Gardens

Old stone sinks make superb mini gardens on a patio or terrace, especially where there is an informal or cottage atmosphere. They are becoming hard to find so go instead for the old glazed butlers pantry-type sinks (though now even they are becoming popular and scarce). It does not matter if they are cracked or chipped, and so, useless for their intended purpose.

Old sinks can always be made to look like stone quite easily: first paint the outside and several inches down the inside with waterproof bonding agent; then, when this has gone sticky apply a layer of hypertufa (two parts sphagnum peat, one part sand and one part cement), adding enough water to make a pliable mix. Spread a layer of about 1.2cm (1/2in) thick, thus creating a rough textured surface to resemble natural

stone. Leave this to harden for two weeks.

To fill the sink, you place broken clay pots (crocks) over the drainage hole, then add more broken clay pots to make a layer about 2.5cm (1in) deep and top this up with a thin layer of rough peat or leafmould. Finally, fill the sink to within 2.5cm (1in) of the top with compost.

You can also use uncracked sinks to make a miniature water garden providing you seal off the drainage hole – this, however, is not necessary should you want to transform your sink into a bog garden (see page 81). Alternatively, use a wooden tub lined with a piece of black butyl-rubber pool liner. Place the tub in a sunny spot on the patio, or if you prefer, sink it into an area left unpaved almost up to its rim, with its edges surrounded by rocks and moisture-loving plants.

## PERMANENT PLANTING IDEAS

We have looked so far at mainly semi-permanent and portable planting ideas, but if you want more permanent planting areas you will have to take these into consideration at the initial planning and building stages of your patio. This is especially true if you want to incorporate some form of water feature (see page 73).

### Double Wall Beds

Double walls are not only decorative features but also are designed for planting. They can be

Fig 79 The choice of plants and materials for the patio can be matched to the style and character of your home: old stone flags and roses round the door are perfect for this classic country cottage.

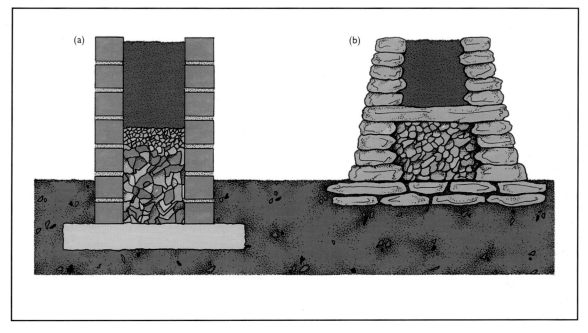

*Fig 80   Narrow raised beds make useful partitions and can be faced in brick, stone or peat blocks to match other patio materials: (a) brick with concrete copings; (b) random stone for a more informal effect.*

built around or in front of a terrace or patio area, and would make an attractive retaining wall for a terrace.

The best width for a double wall is usually 60–75cm (2–2½ft). Build each wall as described in the chapter on patio construction (*see* pages 45–49). You can use bricks, ornamental concrete walling blocks or stone walling blocks, bedding them in with mortar. Cross-ties of stone or iron bars will be needed every 1.2m (4ft) and the tops can be finished off with neat coping stone or bricks. Dry stone walls need no mortar and are built as described in the chapter on Protection (*see* page 49).

To fill the double wall, place a layer of rubble in the bottom for drainage and fill up with a light to medium topsoil. Leave a space for watering at the top. With a dry stone wall, planting holes can be left as you build, so that the plants can protrude from the sides with their roots in the compost-filled middle area.

## Raised Beds

These are ideal for patios as the paved area is a good foundation. You can site the beds in the sun or shade and they can be set against a back wall or be free-standing, thus giving you a great deal of flexibility.

The beds can be made to any shape you desire, square, rectangular or circular or even irregular or curved. The depth should be around 45.5–60cm (18–24in) and make sure drainage holes are left in the sides at ground level. If the soil water stains your paving area, you will have to incorporate some kind of gulley to take it away. This will have to be built at the patio construction stage.

The beds can be built up from bricks, ornamental concrete, walling blocks, lightweight building blocks, logs, second-hand timber railway sleepers or natural stone. The natural stone could be used as dry stone walling which looks very good in a traditional garden setting or the informality of a country cottage garden.

To fill the beds place a layer of rubble or shingle at the bottom for drainage and fill them with a good light to medium topsoil, or use a potting compost. Remember to leave space at the top for watering. If you want to grow lime-hating plants, use an acid topsoil or compost containing plenty of peat or leafmould. If you intend to grow mainly alpines and bulbs, use a very well-drained, gritty compost.

## Rock-Gardens

A rock-garden incorporated into your patio area will help add height and variety as well as provide the opportunity to grow fascinating alpines and heathers. It would be especially useful to incorporate such a feature into the retaining slope of a

*Fig 81 Paving and walling in a matching finish are used to create a variety of levels.*

terrace or patio dug out of a hillside garden. The extent of this feature will depend on the size of area you have – a few rocks piled up in the corner of a suburban sun terrace is not going to produce a realistic or attractive effect.

A rock-garden is really an informal setting of boulders which should, as far as possible, be arranged to simulate a natural formation in the wild, which is why incorporating it into the back slope of a hillside patio – providing it is not very steep – would look particularly good. The rock-garden has to provide sufficient moisture for the needs of alpines in the summer, yet have very good drainage and protection from lying damp in the winter. You can help reduce moisture loss by covering the thin soil between the plants with fine gravel.

Siting the rock-garden in an appropriate place is important and the backdrop should look as natural as possible, this means having not too steep a slope, a hedge or a screen of large shrubs. Man-made backdrops such as walls are not suitable, and this should be borne in mind when deciding if your patio would suit such a feature. Another thing to take into consideration is drainage, for not only does the water have to drain through the rock-garden it will have to be able to drain away.

The type of rocks you use are also important. You will need plenty of wide flat stones in more or less rectangular shapes, rather than those of cubic proportions as you will find it easier to work with these. Try and use local stone as this will look more natural, however, sandstones and limestones are the best types to build with and they weather well. Weathering is important, for the stones need to be fairly porous, with cracks and crevices in which roots of plants can seek coolness and moisture. Impermeable rocks such as granite are inappropriate in a rock-garden, and will also look out of place near most terraces and patio areas. A lot of trial and error will be required to get your rock arrangement looking right. Take your lead from such outcrops in the wild and do not start planting until you are satisfied with the results.

**CHAPTER 6**

# Water on the Patio

Water adds an extra dimension to any size or style of patio. The beauty of pools or simple moving water features such as a fountain or spout is that they can be as large or small as you need, adding light and sparkle to a rather formal scheme, brightening a dull corner or providing wonderful movement and ever-changing reflections. With the patio taking on an increasingly important role as a place to relax, it has long been recognised that water has excellent anti-stress properties. A simple wooden seat close by a small pool or even a wide stone slab constituting part of the coping surround, encourages the lazy observation of fish or the reflection of clouds passing overhead and of the gently waving foliage of nearby plants. The trickle or splash of moving water is also very soothing and a pleasure to observe, cascading over stone, glass or metal, spraying sparkling droplets into the sky or just spilling into a bowl or trough.

## PRACTICAL POINTS

It makes sense to plan any kind of water feature before the patio is installed, to avoid having to dig up your paving or make any other major structural alterations. Also, materials used to conceal the actual pool construction can naturally be matched to and incorporated with those used to build your patio for a fully integrated appearance. However, if the area is already established, it is still perfectly possible to adapt your ideas accordingly, with a raised pool or a free-standing feature. If you want a fountain, spout or cascade, you will need some kind of water pump to recycle the water. The submersible types are neater and more efficient than a surface pump which requires some kind of housing (awkward to conceal on the patio) and more maintenance. A submersible may be more expensive but performs and lasts better. The pump must be of sufficient capacity to cope with the volume of water you wish to move. Your supplier should be able to advise you. One of the larger models can be used to run more than one feature, which is useful if you are planning a sophisticated water complex with a series of pools, weirs and fountains. Ideally, all the necessary electrics, cables and other services should be concealed under the paving.

## POOLS

The patio pool can be any size and shape, for even the tiniest circle or square, big enough for a single miniature water-lily or a few fish, has its own charm and patio appeal. The pool can be sunk into the ground or raised to match raised beds, built-in seating and other timber, stone or brick patio features.

There are several ways of constructing a sunken pool. You can buy a moulded ready-made liner in semi-rigid glass fibre or plastic and sink it into a hole dug roughly the correct size and shape. There should be as few gaps beneath and around the liner as possible, and a lining of sand or damp peat helps it to settle snugly in position. Tough and quick to install, the main disadvantage of the pre-moulded pool is that it limits you in choice of size and shape, although they do come in a fairly wide range of formal and informal shapes and sizes. This may give you problems if you already have

*Fig 82   A large informal pond incorporating rocky falls can make a splendid backdrop to a patio scheme.*

*Fig 83   Containers sunk into the ground and surrounded by timber or pebbles are a simple but effective way to create a pool on the patio.*

firm ideas for the patio, but if you start with the pool and plan your other features around it, it may work very well.

If you prefer to try something of your own design, the easiest method involves strong polyethylene, PVC or butyl-rubber sheeting which can mould itself to any size or shape. These materials come in various grades, the strongest (and most expensive) of which is butyl rubber. Available in a choice of thicknesses, this is extremely tough, resistant to sunlight and can be repaired if punctured. To calculate the length of liner you require, measure twice the depth of your excavated pool plus the length and add 60cm (2ft); the width is twice the depth plus the width and 60cm (2ft); and for an irregular shape, take the maximum measurements. You must check that there are no stones or sharp objects in the hole, and then add a blinding of around 7cm (3in) of fine sand. The liner is placed neatly around the pool and weighted on the banks with bricks or boulders, then water is run gently into the pool using a hosepipe and as it fills, the weight of the water will pull the liner into place. With a stretchable liner such as PVC or butyl this will produce a smooth, crease- and wrinkle-free surface, whilst other, cheaper materials may need coaxing into position.

Pools can also be lined with concrete and while this used to be the traditional method of pool construction and is long lasting and sturdy — costing around the same as a stretchable liner — the extra work involved has made this a less popular choice in recent years. Even with frost-proof additives, concrete is also prone to cracking in winter weather and draining and relining is a tedious task. Some still prefer it as a lining material though, as it cannot be pierced or punctured which is an important consideration if you are constructing something that needs to be sturdy, such as a child's paddling pool. Measurements and installation must be strictly accurate, as there is no leeway for errors and no opportunity to adjust or correct the construction once it is underway. The base and sides of the pool should be at least 15cm (6in) thick and this will

have to be allowed for in your excavations. To estimate the amount of concrete you require, you add up the total area of the base and sides and multiply by the thickness of the concrete, remembering to subtract the thickness of the base from the height of the walls and the thickness of the two walls from the length of the two walls opposite. The concrete mix should be one part cement to two parts sand and three parts coarse aggregate in the form of gravel or crushed stone. These proportions should be accurately measured using a bucket or wheelbarrow. You should not work under frosty conditions, however; a warm day also is not ideal since it causes the concrete to dry out too quickly, making it advisable to lay polythene or wet newspaper over the newly laid surface to retain moisture. Concrete carries on hardening for weeks but you can fill your pool with water after around twenty-four hours, providing you do not stand on the concrete or disturb it for three or four days.

The concrete will need reinforcing with rods or chicken wire which you lay around the base of the pool and up the sides. The base is laid first, making sure there are no air pockets in or around the chicken wire. Timber or hardboard shuttering will be necessary to concrete the sides of a formal-shaped pool. However, you must be careful to prevent the concrete from sticking to the boards by rubbing them with a soapy cloth. Pouring the concrete down between the shuttering and the sides of the pool can be a tricky business, as you have to make sure that the mix is stiff enough not to slump to the bottom. A concrete pool cannot be used straight away as the lime content in the mixture is toxic to plants and fish. The pool will need to be filled and emptied between four and six times over a period of several weeks. If you can't wait that long, there is a special compound which you paint on to the concrete as a sealant. Although this wears off in time, the process is very gradual and there will be no risk by this stage.

Sunken pools can include both formal and informal shapes. The informal, curved pond is ideal for counteracting the harder lines of paving slabs or a square-shaped patio, or for devising a semi-wild corner with natural plants hiding the edges. The most important point to remember when constructing a pool and using any of the lining methods described above, is that the base must be absolutely level. You should use your spirit level and planking at every stage and always double check. A narrow shelf all around the perimeter of the pool about 25–30cm (10–12in) below the proposed level of the water, should be incorporated in your excavations if you are hoping to grow marginal plants (those that like just their roots to be submerged in water). The alternative is to stand the plant pots or baskets on concrete blocks – making sure these have no sharp edges if yours is a plastic-lined pool.

The raised pool is specially suited to the patio. It can be integrated into the general design using the same materials, it adds height and bulk to the scheme and offers the added pleasure of water, plants and fish being easier to observe, especially if seating is designed as part of the pool surround. Because of the pressure of water, a double liner is required and the best type is the butyl rubber or PVC method, as concrete is prone to frost damage. Simple geometric shapes such as squares or rectangles are also recommended for ease of construction, although raised circular pools are possible (see below) or are sometimes available as a completely self-contained unit.

The pool is usually built using bricks or blocks and again, a regular shape makes it easier to calculate and cut materials. To estimate how many bricks you need, you approximate the size of the finished pool and divide the length and width of the structure by the length of one of your intended bricks. It is best to overestimate how many you need to allow for breakages although the width of the mortar joints allows a little flexibility. Doubling the length and width will give you the number of bricks required for a single course, and the total number of courses required is calculated by dividing the height of the pond by the height of a single brick. It may be necessary with a small pool to adjust the dimensions slightly to suit the size of your material to

save awkward cutting. The liner will be tucked into the top course of bricks so this will be the final level of the water; and often the top course is laid on edge for a smarter finish. In this case, you will have to calculate around three times as many bricks for that particular course. The inner wall is calculated in the same way and here it may be better to use cheaper concrete blocks since they will not be seen.

The shape of the pool must be marked out with pegs and string in the same way as you would for a sunken pool. You should check that the corners are true by measuring the diagonal which should be of equal length. It is also worth checking that the sides are parallel with any boundary walls or fences within your patio scheme. The raised pool will require foundations dug to below the level of the topsoil so that the level of the concrete base will be below the surface, and wider than the final width of the walls for stability. Calculate the amount of concrete needed as already described, but use one part cement, two and a half parts sand, five parts coarse aggregate mix. This is simply compacted into the trench and levelled. Pegs are then installed at intervals and checked with a spirit level to ensure accuracy, however, they should be removed before the concrete sets. The containing wall is built in the same way as your patio walls, except that it has a double skin. It is generally easier to build the inner leaf first, providing you have set down at least one course of the outer wall first as this determines the position and size of the finished pool. The trick is to make sure the corners are correctly cemented into place, then lay the rest of the course.

It is important to stagger bricks and blocks so that the joints in each course are positioned to the centre of those above and below. The inner and outer leaves should be tied about every three or four bricks using special wire loops, again staggering these so that they do not line up. The distance between the two leaves depends on the size of your coping material intended for the top.

A small raised circular pond is a slightly different

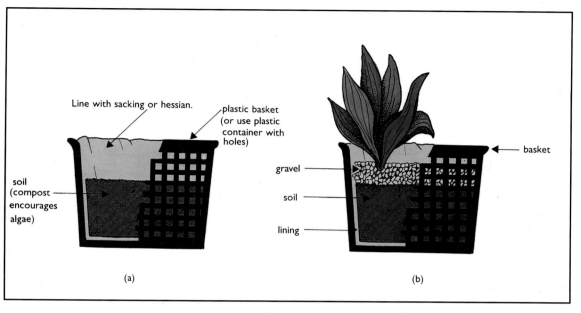

*Fig 84   Marginal and underwater plants are best planted in containers: (a) line a pond basket or old milk crate with sacking or hessian and fill with garden soil; (b) firm in the plant and top with a layer of gravel or shingle to prevent the soil floating away when the basket is submerged.*

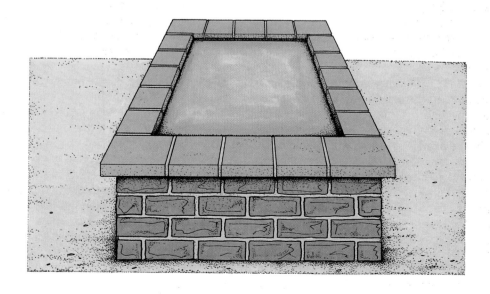

*Fig 85   A raised pool makes a beautiful centre-piece to a formal patio.*

77

affair requiring skill and patience. A separate double leaf wall is not practical as the bricks will not align properly when staggered. Also, if the bricks do not have a curved face, they tend to protrude in alternate courses. This might not show up on a large pond, but will look rather haphazard on a small one. Laying the bricks in alternate header and stretcher courses, or just header courses, will improve the appearance.

The liner is measured and inserted as described before, ensuring that the weight of the water forces it to fit snugly against the structure. Once this is in place, the coping can be put on; you can do this either by laying more bricks at rights angles, or – if you want to use it as a seat or somewhere to stand pots of plants – by using flat coping slabs. If you do not have the time or resources to build a raised pool, you can improvise using an attractive large urn or pot, or an old wooden barrel, providing they are made waterproof. Remember to use a non-toxic sealant if you will be adding fish or plants. These are small but highly effective, and you can maintain them just for the gleam of water or plant them with a single water-lily or an attractive water plant.

## MOVING WATER

Some kind of moving water feature is always particularly appealing as part of a patio scheme. Even the smallest and simplest spout or plume will add life and sparkle, plus it will give that unmistakeably relaxing sound. Many are also highly ornamental, so make a valuable focal point. They can be used to add another dimension to a pool, or be a feature in themselves. A fountain, spout or trickle combined with a shallow bowl of water or concealed reservoir is ideal if the patio is used by young children, since pools can be dangerous. A reservoir in the form of a simple galvanized tank can be concealed beneath your paving slabs and fitted with a submersible pump to recycle the water from an ornamental or bubble fountain. A small grating or grid beneath, allows the

Fig 86  Small fountain spouts are ideal for adding interest, as well as the sound of moving water in a small patio pool.

water to filter through and can be covered with gravel, pebbles, an interesting rock or old millstone.

Display fountains come in many styles and designs from simple spouts and urns to bell shapes, cute figures, fish and cherubs, or the water can be allowed to cascade directly over stones, a brass or stone ball or other natural materials. It is important that the spread and flow of the water is closely calculated, so that it does not overspill on to the patio. Quite apart from the inconvenience, you will be forever topping up the water levels in your reservoir.

Water cascades are equally attractive but require a powerful pump to drive them – it needs to pump at least 40–60lpm (533–800gph). As part of a patio scheme, a formal style looks more in keeping than a natural waterfall with its rocky boulders and wild plants. The formal cascade is easily made by linking two small pools on different levels or by allowing the water to spill between two receptacles such as concrete boxes or bowls. To ensure a good-looking flow that falls directly from one container to another, you will have to experiment with their position and alignment. Tilting them forward slightly helps and so does an angled lip or spout. Again, it is important that the water is not allowed to splash on to the patio surface.

There are also many styles of ornamental waterfall, where the water is encouraged to cascade down a brick wall or similar vertical surface. The wall itself might be ornamental, constructed in coloured brick or designed in curved waves, pillars or angled columns. Sometimes a plain wall can be fitted with aluminium or rust-proof metal fins over which the water cascades, transparent Perspex sheeting, or a slab of slate or stone; all of which can be used instead of brick. Another interesting treatment for walls is the waterspout. Here the water trickles or flows from a simple spout, old tap, head, mask or other ornamental device into a bowl or on to

pebbles and a hidden reservoir below. This is a delightful feature for the small patio, as it takes up the minimum of space yet provides all the pleasure of moving water. With a wall mounted feature, concealing the outlet pipe from the pump can be a problem. The best way is to fit it between the two courses when the wall is first constructed. If the wall is already in existence, it is sometimes possible to remove the coping and thread the pipe through. The alternative is to remove bricks or make a channel through the block wall using a hammer and chisel and replastering it afterwards. It is difficult to make good the damage neatly and it may be better to think of another way of installing the feature – perhaps even by building a new section of wall in front of the original one.

There are free-standing moving water features which can be purchased complete and ready to fit to your pump and water supply. Free-standing

*Fig 87   A simple weir adds the formal effect of moving water and can be fully integrated into a well-planned patio design.*

*Fig 88 Underwater spotlights can be used to illuminate a moving water feature to great effect at night.*

ornamental fountains are usually made from stone, stone effect material or terracotta and maybe even ceramic for milder climates. These comprise a sturdy pedestal, decorative bowl and modest water plume. They make an excellent centre-piece to a patio area and there are also corner-shaped models for smaller areas or where you need a little extra excitement and interest. A similar effect can be found on an even smaller scale fitted into ornamental urns and containers. Oriental-style glazed pots and rough terracotta urns with more of a Mediterranean flavour come complete, fitted with small concealed pump, bed of pebbles, maybe a few plants and a tiny bell or bubble fountain. These could be fitted virtually anywhere: in the centre of a small paved area, on a low wall or as part of an arrangement of similar containers, the others being planted with seasonal or evergreen plants.

The most sophisticated kind of moving water feature and certainly the most expensive is one incorporated into a piece of sculpture. This might be a totally abstract design or comprise a figure or spouting head. Some are witty; some are beautiful; others are stunning in their simplicity and they might be made of stone, marble,

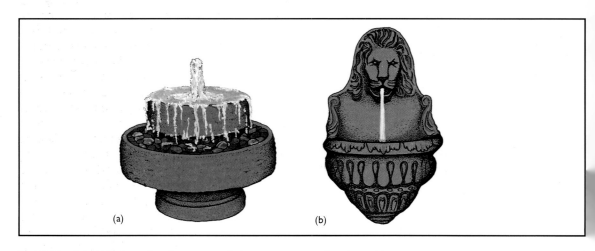

*Fig 89 (a)   A bubble fountain takes up very little space on a small patio and is particularly suitable for families with young children as the water reservoir is completely concealed. (b) Wall fountains can be highly ornamental, and are a delightful way to incorporate running water in the minimum of space.*

bronze, glass, Perspex, metal or a combination of materials. Certainly each is a work of art, usually a limited edition deserving a very special place in your patio scheme. These need not be centre stage, but might take the form of an unexpected feature in a quiet corner or the focal point of a particular area within the patio plan. The right position is vital to the success and enjoyment of garden sculpture. It should look as natural as possible and in some way be linked or integrated with its surroundings. Some pieces are designed to stand alone; others benefit from a backdrop of leafy plants trained across a trellis or the starker effect of a brick wall. The softening effect of large, architectural plants positioned near the sculpture in pots and containers, and arranged so that they semi-envelop it, will often look superb and can blend the piece beautifully with its outdoor environment. This also helps disguise necessary pipework and connections. A water sculpture is usually designed to be stood in a pool or over a hidden reservoir with pebbles, gravel or boulders at the base to disguise it.

## BOG GARDENS

A small bog garden offers the opportunity to grow a fascinating selection of plants, many of which have exotically shaped foliage and flowers to produce an area of special interest on the patio. It offers all the excitement of marginal species without the labour and inconvenience involved in building a pool. It is completely safe for children too. Bog plants enjoy badly drained water-logged soil – an environment that is easily created in a small container, such as an old stone sink or old barrel with a few holes drilled in the base. If you have more space available, a series or group of such containers, maybe slightly sunk into the ground and planted with different plants, can look very attractive. Otherwise, a shallowly dug area – maybe the size of one or two removed paving slabs – can be lined with punctured PVC or butyl rubber to produce a suitable environment. Ideally, around 7.5cm (3in) of water should stand on top of the soil and a high level of moisture be maintained by topping up with a hose when required. A highly efficient way of doing this is to insert a section of plastic pipe in the bottom of the container before it is planted, punching holes in the pipe at intervals and leaving the other end of the pipe exposed on top of the soil. This can be hidden behind foliage when the container is planted. Thus, the bog garden is particularly suited to damp, shadier patios where the soil is likely to stay saturated longer. There may be some water overspill in rainy weather, therefore it is an advantage to semi-recess your containers in the ground and surround them with pebbles.

Fig 90 A beautifully designed and planted informal pool, well sheltered by a trellis and with seating close by from which to enjoy the effect.

81

## WATER FOR PLEASURE

If there is no room in the garden for a swimming pool, you may still have room in your patio plans for a fun water feature such as a hot tub, spa or splash pool. Because the water is hot, these can be used most seasons of the year – even with snow on the ground – providing the area is well sheltered; so, in many ways, these offer far better value than a pool. The bubbling, massaging effect of the water is supposed to have therapeutic effects too. A hot tub is simply a deep wooden barrel with a round base and straight sides, usually made from rot-resistant redwood, teak or cedar. Other shapes are available but less common, including square, rectangular or even hexagonal styles. You sit in it up to your neck in massaging jets of hot water. The water is circulated and recycled by means of a centrifugal pump which sucks water out at the base and forces it through a filtration system, heating it on the way. It re-enters at the top and sides via hydro jets or air blower producing powerful jets of moving water. A hot tub can be recessed or free-standing but should be well sheltered, not just for privacy but for comfort too. Plenty of large leafy plants look good against natural timber, and bamboo or wicker screens will provide a relaxing jungle atmosphere. Because the tubs are wooden, they look particularly good set in or on a timber-decked patio. Fibreglass spa pools are less expensive but they come in a variety of shapes and sizes which are not as attractive to look at and must be built into your paving or decking.

The splash pool is more of a summer-only feature – a kind of substitute for a full-scale swimming pool – although they are frequently integrated into a larger pool design. However, as a feature alone, they still provide hours of pleasure for both adults and children and can be easily fitted on to or butted up to a larger sized patio. The minimum size pool is normally around 3 × 4m (10 × 13ft) with a depth of water of about 90cm (36in). It requires the same heating and filtration facilities as a swimming pool, so these will need to be concealed nearby, and a locking stout wooden lid is a good idea when not in use. This will not only conserve water heat and be safer with young children around, but could double, with the addition of a few mats or cushions, as a sunbathing platform or play area. If children will be using the pool, it is a good idea to site it close to the house, so that they can be observed from the kitchen or sitting room window. The splash pool is usually sunk into the ground and neatly bordered with tiles, bricks, paving or timber to match your patio.

*Fig 91 A pond or bog garden is the perfect opportunity to grow some exciting water-loving foliage plants.*

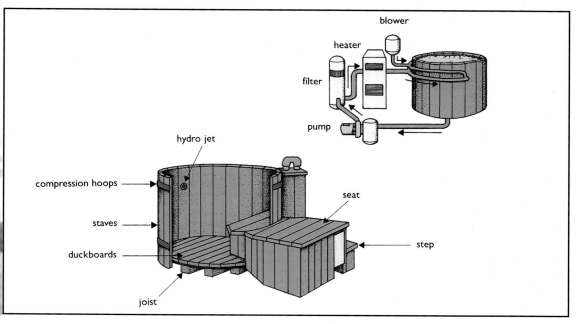

Fig 92  A hot tub works by circulating and recycling the water using a
centrifugal pump, which sucks the water out at the bottom and forces it
through a filtration system and heater before returning it to the top.
Hydro jets or an air blower produce a bubbling, stimulating effect.

When considering a spa or hot tub for the patio, you should first select a site that can be well sheltered and which is easy and convenient to use from the house. Ideally, it should be close by a patio, dining or lounging area and surrounded by trellises, screens or other forms of windproof protection. Overhead shelter is also a good idea in the shape of a pergola structure with bamboo blinds or similar framework.

These water features are heavy – when full of water and bathers, a tub might weigh anything up to 3,628kg (8,000lb), so it is essential to check that the site and your planned paving material is strong enough to take it. This is especially important if the feature is to be installed as part of a roof garden patio. A reinforced concrete slab about 15cm (6in) thick should be sufficient or you could support the tub on reinforced concrete piers or wooden joists. You will probably want to use your tub or spa in the evenings, so plan for the area to be lit too (see page 24).

Once these requirements are met, they are not difficult to install. Many tubs and spas are available in kit form ensuring that the necessary pump, heater, filter and hydro jet system are compatible, and simply need connecting to the appropriate services. You can also buy optional extras such as bubble effects, insulated covers, steps and platforms. You should follow the same hygiene and safety precautions for hot tubs, spas or splash pools as you would for swimming pools: that is, avoid slippery surfaces such as natural stone underfoot in the vicinity; follow strictly the chemical and filtration treatments as recommended by the manufacturer; never allow children to use the feature unattended; and do not allow glassware in or near the area. Other practical points are common sense: such as to organize the surrounding patio area so that loose material such as gravel, chippings, leaves and other debris cannot be trodden into the area; and never to allow animals into the water.

# CHAPTER 7

# Decorating the Patio

The successful and good-looking patio relies on those final touches such as garden ornaments and other purely decorative items, like any well furnished 'room'. These might only be small, perhaps something a bit different to add a touch of character and originality or a novelty used to brighten a dull corner or liven up a low wall.

Fig 93 Look out for unusual garden items like this atmospheric wickerwork figure.

Alternatively, the feature could be quite dominant within your scheme, making an excellent focal point or special area of interest. Outdoor accessories are also useful for reinforcing, sometimes even creating, a theme or atmosphere, for example, you might want to adopt an oriental style or a Mediterranean feel. Just two or three items could be enough to suggest such a theme, if carefully chosen and thoughtfully placed. In spring and summer, they may be beautifully displayed in conjunction with foliage and flowers, which are used either to semi-disguise them and soften their effect, so that they look like an inseparable part of the scheme or positioned and trained to set them off. The living shapes and colours of the plants will create a backdrop or framework for a fine feature.

Position is important when adding even small objects, if they are to have the intended effect. A good prominent spot is required for objects you wish to be the key point of your scheme or to catch the eye. This is often the way a free-standing fountain, a fine statue or ornamental urn is best displayed. Centre stage is always guaranteed to grab the attention immediately, and in a formal patio design which radiates out from a central point, some form of decorative focal point is necessary. Ornaments can be given extra impact by raising them closer to eye level on a plinth or column. Small objects may be displayed on a table, trellis, fence-mounted brackets or wall. Sometimes a symmetrical

Fig 94 (Opposite) Classic sculptures look superb against dark greenery – a large piece like this would look splendid on even the smallest patio, if given the right setting.

*Fig 95 (a) A stone-crafted basket of fruit. (b) Oriental-style lanterns, buddhas and pagodas are useful where you are trying to create an authentic Japanese atmosphere. (c) A wide range of small animal figures are available, to be positioned at the base of pots, on walls or by the side of an ornamental pool. (d) Ornamental water spouts come in a wide choice of figures and styles, like this large cherub pouring water from a jug.*

arrangement of a matching or similar pair of items looks effective, positioned on either side of a flight of steps or doorway. This is a useful way to emphasize the entrance to the house, an archway or formal steps down to the rest of the garden from a patio or terrace. Your ornaments can be made of virtually any weather-proof material such as wood, stone, reconstituted stone, metal, ceramic or terracotta, and they can be chosen to co-ordinate or contrast with patio paving materials and containers.

Garden centres and specialist garden shops can tempt you with a wide variety of outdoor ornaments from life-size statues of nymphs or animals, to sundials, urns, amphora, decorative pots, Chinese ginger jars and terracotta baskets. However, for an instantly mature mellow look, you could scour the auctions and antique shops for antique ornaments such as wonderful stone or lead statuary or ancient urns already covered

in moss, as well as recycled paving slabs, stone or metal seats and well-weathered sundials. Garden sculpture is also guaranteed to add an instant touch of class, a small piece need not be too expensive and could transform your patio scheme into something really special. There is always the thought that original art is a good investment, and some people like to maintain a changing collection, buying and selling new items as they appeal and keeping their patio looking fresh and original. Like any ornament, the right position is vital to ensure the piece looks as much part of the natural environment as possible (*see* page 81).

Of course, eye-catching or decorative items for the garden need cost you nothing at all if you have the knack for spotting an interesting shape or texture in a natural or abandoned object. Rocks, pebbles and stones of all sizes are popular for a great many ornamental roles on the patio and are used extensively and to great effect in oriental schemes. A variety of subtly coloured small pebbles can be positioned below plants in tubs and planting beds to cover the bare soil and help conserve moisture. Larger stones can form an important element in a moving water feature. Larger slabs of rock might be as arresting as a piece of sculpture, equally deserving of a prime position. Indeed, pieces of driftwood, bleached like bone or an interesting lump of wood with a particularly fine bark or knotty distortions could also make a fine centre-piece. Any object might capture your imagination as a suitable patio ornament, even an old basket or wooden cartwheel, a disused millwheel or mangle.

Sometimes plants themselves take on an ornamental role not just through the shape and colour of their flowers and foliage — although it is true that some of the large architectural species like Fatsia japonica or bamboo are as dramatic or elegant as any sculpture — but from the way they have been clipped or trained. Vigorous, fast-growing evergreen climbers like ivy are sometimes trained over wire frames or wooden supports to create living green statues or geometric shapes. Slower-growing evergreen shrubs like box and privet can be clipped into smart geometric topiary shapes such as pyramids, orbs, spirals and cubes and they look particularly good planted in ruddy terracotta pots or smart wooden Versailles planters. These are frequently arranged in formal pairs either side of steps or an entrance or simply arranged in groups of different shapes and sizes.

Then there are all the temporary patio accessories that come out when the weather is

*Fig 96   A large basket used to display an interesting variety of foliage plants.*

Fig 97  Plants can also serve as ornaments when decoratively clipped into shapes and organized into an arrangement of complementary containers.

fine and can be chosen as carefully as any interior furnishings. These might include large floor cushions for lounging or sitting on or smaller versions for softening hard garden benches, and bright patio umbrellas to fix on to the patio table and keep off the midday sun. For alfresco dining you can use cloths, cutlery and china, rugs, awnings, drinks trolleys and all manner of items designed to bring greater comfort to the outdoor environment. Most of these will have to be brought indoors at the end of the day, so convenient storage nearby in the house, conservatory or garage is essential.

## SPECIAL EFFECTS

Although not strictly ornaments, some of the trick effects that can be employed on the patio are highly ornamental. Mirrors are a wonderful way of making a small space look twice the size

or even infinite if you line one up to face another. They look particularly effective set into a fake archway, doorway or behind a trellis. It is important though to remember that a mirror should be placed to reflect something interesting, not just a blank wall or you are only doubling up your dull features. The greatest effect of space is produced where a mirror reflects the image of an entrance or pathway, or some other promise of a vista or garden beyond.

Other illusions can be created with painted *trompe l'oeil* effects (which means literally 'trick of the eye'). Lots of white paint is the simplest and one of the most effective ways of suggesting the impression of light and space in a dark gloomy backyard enclosed by high walls. If your artistic talents stretch a little further than this, you can add realistic-looking plants and trees to bleak corners where nothing will grow or use murals to transform a large expanse of wall into a beautiful parkland vista.

CHAPTER 8

# Patio Furniture

Furniture is a vital element of the finished patio or terrace: after all, somewhere to sit and enjoy the fresh air and view the rest of the garden is one of its prime reasons for existence. You will at least need a seat or bench on which to sit for five minutes peace and quiet. And some kind of table and chairs will enable you to eat outside – you'll find this an irresistible temptation once your patio is finished, so you may as well plan to cater for it, even on the smallest balcony or backyard. Yet patio furniture does not just satisfy your practical needs, it is also important for adding style and to reinforce your planned look and atmosphere. Therefore, it is worth taking time over choosing the right kind of furniture, both for practical purposes and for overall appearance.

For as long as there have been gardens there have been garden seats and it is worth looking at

*Fig 98   The traditional garden seat, mellowed to an unobtrusive pewter grey, provides all-weather seating.*

the history of this vital piece of furniture as many of the old ideas are worth copying; while reproductions of traditional styles are still widely available. Medieval garden seats were little more than a development of the grass bank: simple earth mounds covered with turf or sometimes a bed of low-growing herbs such as thyme or chamomile. The idea was that the crushed herbs gave off a sweet fragrance as you sat down. These simple seats can easily be incorporated into a raised bed area on the patio, though instead of turf or herbs, which might be too damp for thin twentieth-century clothes, you could lay a stone paving slab or place wooden struts across. These could be treated or painted to add a contrast to the natural flower beds on either side.

Because of the dampening effect of turf seats, garden seats soon became the province of the carpenter and stonemason. In fact, by the mid-nineteenth century, stone or marble seats had become very grand. There was a strong interest at this time in Italian formal gardens and the seats reflected this, being in classic semi-circular styles. However, the days must have been very warm to sit on one of these marble beauties for a long time. Some of the less classical stone seats can still be found in architectural salvage yards but they are probably expensive and would only suit a really grand terrace.

Shade from the sun, wind and rain became something of a priority over the centuries and garden seats were often provided with a roof. The earliest form, and the most well known, being the arbour, with climbing plants trailing over the lattice work sides. If you have a big enough patio area a modern-day arbour can be easily constructed using cut, sawn and finished timber, and incorporating the seat in the structure. However, a rustic type of arbour can be made and an appropriately similar style bench purchased to fit under it. If you use rustic poles, the lengths should be nailed together with galvanized nails, flat on the ground before erection. The construction of this is similar to pergolas and arches (*see* page 54).

Seats were also sited so that nature could provide the shade, such as the classic seats built round the trunk of a tree. These can be easily constructed today by anyone competent at woodwork or bought from one of the specialist timber companies. Other forms of shelter for seats was provided by recessing into clipped hedges or shrubs like ancient yew. To be large enough, the specimens would have to be very well established, possibly several hundred years old and unless you have inherited a garden with such mature boundaries, you would have to wait a long time before your seat would be adequately sheltered. But you could reproduce the effect by building a wire or timber framework and growing a vigorous evergreen climber over it.

The nineteenth century also saw the development of the rustic cast-iron seat, with the legs made to resemble branches of trees and shrubs or serpents and snakes. Most of these cast-iron Victorian garden chairs and seats incorporated wooden seats and backs in the form of laths. The elaborate cast-iron ends became very intricate. There are companies producing accurate reproductions of these types of seats, and even the more simple 'park bench' varieties can look very attractive on the right kind of patio.

Some of the real classic designs are also readily available, and being reproduced on a commercial scale. For instance, you can easily purchase the clean-lined timber 'Lutyens' bench seat which looks well on a classic-styled terrace or patio, especially against a background of mellow brick or curtained greenery. To recapture the comfort and elegance of a more leisurely age, there are also wooden wheeled loungers which have that luxurious as well as traditional feel and are available in reproduction forms of original designs.

If you want to make your own patio seat and want to be able to stay outside in all weathers, then the best way is to construct a simple wooden bench from treated timber. Even the simplest built item will at least be a custom-built item and add some element of uniqueness to your finished patio. A simple garden bench can be constructed using two pieces of pine or

Fig 99   Built-in bench-type seating for the fully integrated patio.

Fig 100   Stylish ornamental garden seats in classic style.

hardwood about 20 × 3.7cm (8 × 1½in) nominal size and no more than 1.2m (48in) long. These can be bolted to a pair of painted mild steel support frames of 5 × 0.6cm (2 × ¼in) section.

A more ambitious garden seat with back support can be made using a framework of nominal 6.2 × 3.7cm (2½ × 1½in) section clad with seven rails of 10 × 3.2cm (4 × 1¼in) in section. With rails this size, the seat can be up to 1.5m (5ft) long. Three frames are required and each pair of legs is joined with a halving joint. Bolts and timber connectors are used for jointing to the top horizontal member. The legs are stiffened with either cross or longitudinal members or both. Before the cladding rails are screwed to the framework, they should have their edges rounded off.

There is more to patio furniture than just garden seats. To eat alfresco, you will need a table as well as comfortable dining chairs, then you may also like to relax in the sun (or shade) on a sunbed or lounger. The most comfortable styles of modern furniture for soaking up the sun are not suitable for keeping outside, even on damp summer days, as it tends to be fully upholstered, so if you go for this type of portable furnishing, you will have to have somewhere to store it. Much of this poolside-style furniture is made from moulded plastic, with a dazzling choice of different fabric covers for the comfortable cushions. It usually comes in sets of co-ordinating pieces that could include a mobile reclining chair, sun lounger, bar trolley, foot-stool, low table and six-way positionable chairs. Some of the more up-market types of modern outdoor furniture come with wooden frames rather than moulded plastic, and these can look more stylish on the patio or terrace. A very durable resin, usually in white, is another material that is often used; this is particularly useful for making large tables of any shape and matching outside dining chairs. Most often these chairs will come with cushioned seats and backs which can be removed to clean. However, even with this type of material you are better off storing it away in the winter. At the cheapest end of the market, moulded plastic and aluminium frame dining

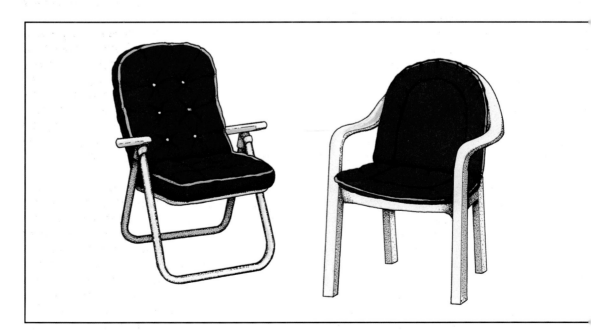

*Fig 101  Upholstered patio furniture combines good looks and comfort.*

*Fig 102 Bamboo and cane furniture is for fine weather use only but looks charming on the patio.*

furniture is lightweight and stackable and can be quite stylish and comfortable for the price, especially if you add your own cushions. All these types of furniture will be available from department stores or garden centres. While we are on the subject of portable garden furniture, don't forget the good old deck-chair. Today, most come with attractively patterned fabrics (or you can cover an old frame with your own choice) and although they are very simple in concept, can sometimes look better on the patio than many gaudy modern plastic types at the cheaper end of the market.

The modern seats and matching tables that are now available in a variety of different designs are more durable. They usually take the form of a simple park bench-style seat with wooden slats and wrought iron sides and legs, plus a table with wrought iron supports and wooden slatted tops. The wrought iron is rust-proofed and finished with a polyester coating that should ensure it can overwinter on the patio. The woodwork on these modern garden seats now comes in many different paint colours as well as natural stained wood finish, and this can liven up the patio giving it up-to-the-minute impact yet a traditionally stylish feel.

If you are lucky enough to have an old piece of marble, say from an old wash-stand cabinet, or happen to know where you can get one cheap, then you could have a fairly unique garden table. This can be made using the marble slab as the top and having a wrought iron or timber base made to measure for you. Other pieces of patio furniture can be improvised using an old scrubbed pine table, folding chairs or even barrels.

If you want to create a rustic look on the patio and don't want to be bothered to bring the furniture indoors over winter, then you can purchase a basic trestle table or the classic park 'picnic tables' which comprise a table and benches built into one unit. Alternatively, either style is quickly made yourself with minimum experience. Your basic garden table should be large enough to accommodate the whole family or maximum number of friends likely to sit round it on a regular basis, yet it should not take up too

Fig 103   An elegant bamboo lounger surrounded by plants creates an
atmosphere of its own in a corner of a much larger patio.

Fig 104   Stone furniture can be left outdoors on the patio all year round.
However, an umbrella is a useful summer addition.

*Fig 105   Timber bench, patio table and simple picnic bench with built-in seating.*

much space on a small patio. In this case you could make a table that will dismantle or partly fold away. The top should be at a comfortable height in relation to the chairs that are to be used, anything between 65–73cm (26–29in) will probably be satisfactory. A simple design involves a top of 15 × 3.7cm (6 × 1½in) planks set with a 2cm (¾in) gap between each, and supported on two or three leg frames of 6.2 × 3.7cm (2½ × 1½in) section. The lower part of each leg frame should be braced to the next by a central longitudinal member.

The average picnic table is slightly more ambitious but will be a strongly made structure. The four main support legs should be 10 × 3.7cm (4 × 1¼in), and the main cross-pieces supporting the seats at each end should be the same measurements. The pair of cross-pieces supporting the strips forming the table top and the seat can be of lighter construction — the same as for the simple table described earlier. The other two main timbers are the V-shaped cross-supports and the pair of cross-pieces supporting the strips of the table top. These should all be 10cm (4in)

wide and 0.5cm (1in) thick. The table top is of similar construction to the one mentioned earlier, but in this case you could use smaller planks, say 10 × 2.5cm (4 × 1in). You will need only two of these on the seats leaving a gap of 5cm (2in).

As this table has to be strong, screws and bolts are used instead of nails. Nearly all the woodwork should be screwed, and the four main legs held by coach bolts. The bolts, after the holes have been drilled for them, should be put through from the inside so that clothes are not snagged on them. On the outside a washer should be used under the bolt and nut, and any surplus bolt should then be cut off when tight and filed down well to a smooth surface.

It is a good idea to leave the base of the four legs untrimmed until the whole table is finished. Then it is possible to stand it up and make a horizontal scribe mark across the base of each one before the final sawing. Another slight alternative to this picnic table is to extend the seating length on each side so that tall people can sit on the seat extension without the need to put their legs under the table.

# CHAPTER 9

# Barbecues

With your patio completed and specially designed to your own specifications, you will be keen to get out and use it to the full. You should be able to treat it as an extension of your home, an outside room where you can enjoy living simply in the sun. It naturally follows that living alfresco means meals outdoors, and rather than just preparing salads and sandwiches in the kitchen to be taken out, you can equip yourself with a full-scale outdoor kitchen by installing a barbecue on the patio.

If your only experience of barbecuing has been to stand with streaming eyes over a smoking oil drum attempting to cook burgers and sausages which persist in turning black and dropping into the flames, then you may well be put off using this form of cooking on your brand new patio. However, tackled correctly, barbecue cooking is great fun and the sampling of it delicious. If you don't fancy the challenge of cooking outdoors on a simple bed of glowing coals, you will find many new, efficient barbecue units fired by bottled gas

*Fig 106   A simple built-in brick or ornamental stone barbecue, using a standard kit which generally includes metal base plate, charcoal grid and food grill.*

Fig 107 A stone built barbecue can be incorporated into the patio as part of the general scheme and built from matching or contrasting stone.

and allowing you as much control as your kitchen cooker – plus there is the exciting option of special grilling and rotisserie features. The secret of successful barbecuing is to know how to control the heat and to get the right equipment for the job. For instance, it is no good trying to cope with a simple little Hibachi type if you want to cook for twenty people or so; but if there are just two of you, you'll not need a great American-size kettle barbecue, big enough to take a family-size turkey.

Today, barbecues can range from a simple grid over glowing coals to a gas-fired mini-furnace, complete with rotisserie, utensils rack, storage cupboard and preparation counter. These sophisticated machines are very easy to use, but they are expensive, so will only be worth the investment if you intend to use one frequently. A basic home-made barbecue can be built as a permanent patio feature and an integrated part of your scheme which saves space on a small patio or offers scope for a complete eating/cooking complex on a large one. For the simplest type of barbecue, all you need to do is build a three-sided brick structure about waist height and four foot long with one rack to hold charcoal and another to hold food. These racks are now very easy to come by from most garden centres and DIY superstores, following the popularity of barbecues over the last decade. You can get whole DIY kits that come with a baseplate to collect ash, and charcoal grids. Some more up-market kits even come with steel-fire box, adjustable height cooking grill and rotisserie brackets.

If you don't want the barbecue to be a permanent structure on the patio, try designing one that can be built quickly and dismantled just as easily. Solid concrete blocks are ideal for this (don't use the lightweight varieties for although they are easy to lift they will break up in the heat). The ideal size of concrete block is 22.8 × 22.8 × 30.5cm (9 × 9 × 12in). For a very basic model, you will need about eight blocks, but you can use as many as you like to get the design you want — you can increase the height by stacking the blocks or you can use them to provide a larger worksurface. You will also need a 5 × 5cm (2 × 2in) thick paving slab 0.6 × 1m (2 × 3ft) to act as the hearth. The cooking grid can then be slotted over the top.

If you want a permanent barbecue and you are going to entertain outdoors a great deal during the summer, then you should look at more sophisticated designs and where to site them. For instance, your patio probably runs out from the kitchen or dining room and there could be unattractive, but functional constructions to hide like central heating tanks or dustbins. So here, you might want to conceal the poor view and

provide shelter by building a back wall to the barbecue. Alternatively, you may wish to make the barbecue a central feature of the patio and the ideal way to do this is to have a circular type. This has the fire and cooking grid in the centre with a wedge-shape cut out in the brick-work to allow easy access. The work-top should be large enough to take a good spread of food, and allow friends and family to gather round. It is worth remembering that the size can be varied but the diameter should not be less than 2m (6½ft) as this will cause problems with bricklaying.

If you have your patio some distance from the house, say by a summer house, swimming pool or just overlooking a beautiful view, you probably will not want the barbecue to be the focal point, so you will have to assess the best place to position it; say leading on from a raised bed or seating. Shelter may also be important, so consider building a wall that will give the feeling of enclosure, yet at the same time not distract from the fine setting of the patio and its view.

If you are going for the permanent barbecue structure, you need to make sure that the brickwork looks good, so you should follow bricklaying instructions very carefully. Brickwork must always be laid to a 'bond' that ensures vertical joints do not coincide. 21.5cm (9in) walls are made up of a combination of bricks laid along (stretchers) and through the wall (headers). There are various bonds such as Flemish and English garden walling (see page 47) that use different combinations of brick patterns. At the end of the wall or at a corner, you need what is called a 'queen- closer' to adjust the bond. This is a cut brick measuring about 5.6cm (2¼in) on a Flemish bond.

The initial course is vital. If this is correctly positioned, then the subsequent courses will be far easier. So, to lay this first course, mark out a chalk line using a builder's line coated with chalk. It is pulled tight and snapped so that a chalk impression is transferred to the footing below.

Use a mix of three parts soft sand to one part cement and a small amount of plasticizer. Start at

*Fig 108   A more decorative circular built-in barbecue incorporating a useful wide, flat surface for seating and serving.*

*Fig 109   (a) The last word in sophistication: a trolley gas grill complete with extra burner, temperature gauge, warming rack, lid and storage facilities. (b) The simplest free-standing barbecues are inexpensive and easy to pack away when not in use.*

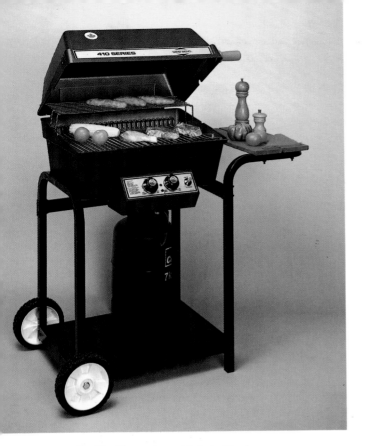

*Fig 110   The most sophisticated barbecues are gas powered and include all kinds of special cooking facilities.*

the end of one wall and bed in a brick in a layer of mortar 1cm thick. Lay a second brick 1m (3ft) away and check the level between the two with a straight-edge and spirit-level. Continue until the first course is complete, then build up the corners four to five bricks high, checking the level and plumb with a spirit-level. Next comes the second course, and to do this insert pins round the corners of the brickwork and stretch a builder's line between them, ensuring the line remains taught. The next difficulty is to judge the thickness of the mortar bed between each course. This can be overcome by making a simple gauge with a length of wood, marking on the depth of each course.

It is worth remembering that if you are building a circular barbecue the shape produces a greater inherent strength and here you can use a single brick of 11.2cm (4½in). The types of brick that you use is entirely up to you, as there are now so many attractive colours readily available. However, you must remember to use a hard, frost-resistant brick and also hard engineering bricks should be used where it will be subjected to heat from the barbecue.

When the bricklaying is finished the next step is pointing the walls and the barbecue. The most attractive way to do this is to scrape out the cement to a depth of about 4cm (1½in). The walls of the barbecue will obviously surround a cavity where the fire or barbecue appliance is to fit, so the bottom will have to be infilled. This is best done with clean hardcore which can be covered with ash or sharp sand and then bricks or frost-free tiles used to complete the work.

If you really don't want to go to all the trouble of building your own barbecue structure, even a removable one, then you should look at the portable types that can be seen in most garden centres and DIY superstores. The first stage is usually only a little Hibachi-type on legs. The bowl can be round or square and usually the legs are removable. The more expensive ones have a kettle-type cooker and draught-control system built in to the bowl. This makes cooking more efficient. These models with lids act as a conventional oven and mean you can smoke large pieces of meat such as a turkey. Right at the top end of the market, you'll find the power-assisted barbecue where burning is helped along by gas or electricity. These machines are usually mounted on a trolley and may have a spit, cooking table or shelves built on. They even have exotic gadgets like a corn roaster, baked potato accessory or kebab attachment. Some are charcoal fired but the gas or electric powered models use reusable rocks over the burners. The flavour of food is the same as when cooking by charcoal.

You can still have an electric or gas powered barbecue built in to your own design as long as you remember to site it near a power supply for electricity or somewhere to hide the propane gas bottles. You will also have to get your dimensions right so that these models fit your construction. As well as the barbecue, you will also need a set of long-handled cooking tools and some good heatproof gloves.

Lighting-up time is easy with the up-market gas and electric models, but if you want to be natural with a real charcoal model, there are a few rules to make sure everything cooks at the proper temperature and without clouds of smoke. Firstly, charcoal driven models should be sited in a sheltered area as wind makes the charcoal flare. Buying good quality charcoal will make lighting up easier. It comes in several forms, including chips, which are pieces of charcoal wood, and will need the help of a barbecue starter – never use

methylated spirit, paraffin, petrol or kindling – to light up and be ready for cooking in about fifteen minutes. Treated chips will light on their own and need about ten minutes heating up time. Briquettes are harder to light than chips, always need the help of a fire-lighter or a barbecue starter, and they take up to thirty minutes to reach cooking stage, but they do burn longer than chips. A fuel to beware of, is the large cheap bags of charcoal which contain a mixture of wood, briquettes and broken coal. Lastly, do not attempt to use wood, house coal and peat, as they are not suitable fuels.

*Fig III   Where space is limited and the barbecue only used occasionally, a wheel-away model may be the most practical choice.*

*Fig 112  A sheltered barbecue complex.*

The next rule is to arrange your charcoal in the barbecue with a fire-lighter, making sure there is an air space beneath. If you are using one of the manufacturer's paste or liquid starter fuels follow the instructions carefully.

Now that the fire is lit, cooking can begin. Here again, there are some simple tips to follow if you want to get away from the 'take it off when it's black' method of barbecuing. First bring the coals to the right temperature, then sprinkle them with herbs or aromatic wood chips for extra flavour. Oil the grill to prevent food sticking. If you are planning to make kebabs, marinate them first using a mixture of equal quantities of olive oil and lemon juice with a generous pinch of fresh or dried thyme or marjoram. Marinate for at least eight hours to make the meat tender. Other meats should be trimmed of fat and brushed with melted butter or vegetable oil. Chops can also benefit from marinating. Try not to over-crowd the grill, as too much fat can drip on the coals and cause clouds of smoke. If you are

intending to use a baste or glaze this should be brushed on towards the end of the cooking time.

Barbecues that provide closed cooking act more like a conventional oven so you should follow manufacturer's instructions and timings carefully. If you want baked potatoes or corn cobs to go with the grilled food, wrap them in a double layer of oiled foil and place them amongst the coals. Potatoes take about an hour, corn about fifteen minutes. If you own a microwave oven you could cook the potatoes in this first and finish them off with ten minutes on the grid to crisp the skins.

After the party is over and you've finished cooking, the barbecue must be safely extinguished. Air vent models with a lid will go out if you close the vent and put the cover on. Once the coals are cold, you can empty them and clean the bowl and grid. Coals can be extinguished with earth or sand on an open barbecue. Dousing with water is not really satisfactory or recommended.

# BARBECUE RECIPES

## Meet Dishes

### Meat Dishes

*Indian-Style Kebabs*

Serves 4–6

1lb minced beef
1 garlic clove, crushed
2.5cm (1in) fresh ginger root, peeled and chopped
1½ teaspoons paprika
1 tablespoon strong curry powder
½ tablespoon ground coriander
pinch of chilli powder
salt and freshly ground pepper
1 egg beaten
juice of ½ lemon

**For the yogurt sauce:**
¼ pint of natural yogurt
salt
4 fresh mint leaves, chopped, or 1 teaspoon of dried mint
¼ teaspoon of clear honey
1 garlic clove, crushed
1 teaspoon dried fenugreek leaves
½ teaspoon of ground coriander or 1 teaspoon of chopped fresh coriander leaves
freshly ground pepper
1 tablespoon sunflower oil

Put the minced meat into a large mixing bowl and add the garlic, ginger, ½ teaspoon of paprika, the curry powder, coriander, chilli powder and seasoning. Mix well and work in the beaten egg. Set aside for 5 minutes. Mould the mixture into long, thin shapes around 4–6 greased skewers.

To make the yogurt sauce, mix all the ingredients together in a bowl and sprinkle with ½ teaspoon of the paprika. Set aside until ready to serve.

Cook the kebabs over the barbecue for 15 minutes, turning frequently, or until browned and cooked through. Sprinkle with the lemon juice and the rest of the paprika and serve with the yogurt sauce.

*Lamb Patties*

Serves 4–8

1½lb finely minced lean lamb
salt and freshly ground pepper
1 tablespoon chopped fresh mint or 2 teaspoons dried mint
2 tablespoons milk
8 streaky bacon rashers, rinds removed

Mix the lamb with the seasoning, mint and milk and divide the mixture into 8 square patties. Place in the refrigerator to chill for 1 hour, wrapped in greaseproof paper.

Wrap a rasher of bacon around each pattie and fix firmly with a small skewer. Cook over the fire for about 20 minutes, turning once.

*Chicken Yakitori*

Serves 4

4 tablespoons golden syrup
4 tablespoons soy sauce
2 tablespoons dry white wine
1½ teaspoons grated fresh ginger root or ½ teaspoon ground ginger
1 garlic clove, crushed
4 chicken breasts, skinned, boned and cut into 3.75cm (1½in) cubes

Mix together the syrup, soy sauce, wine, ginger and garlic in a shallow dish. Add the chicken pieces, turning to coat them well, then cover and marinate in the refrigerator for 8 hours or overnight, turning the chicken pieces occasionally (however, you don't have to keep getting up through the night!).

Thread the chicken on to 4 skewers and cook over the barbecue for about 10 minutes, turning frequently and brushing with the marinade until the chicken is tender and browned.

## Fish Dishes

### Red Mullet with Fennel

Serves 4

4 red mullet, cleaned and washed
6–8 fennel sprigs
olive oil
juice of 1 lemon
lemon wedges

Score the fish lightly on each side with a sharp knife. Reserve 2 tablespoons of chopped fennel leaves and chop up the remaining leaves finely with the stalks. Lay the fish on a double thickness of foil and stuff them with some of the fennel, laying the rest of it between the fish. Sprinkle with olive oil and some of the lemon juice. Cook over the fire for about 20–30 minutes, brushing with oil and lemon juice occasionally.

To garnish the dish, sprinkle the fish with the reserved fennel and serve with lemon wedges.

### Barbecued Salmon Steaks

Serves 4

4 salmon steaks
4 tablespoons olive oil or sunflower oil
1 teaspoon chopped fresh rosemary or ½ teaspoon dried rosemary
salt and freshly ground white pepper
fresh rosemary sprigs
4 lemon wedges

Lay the salmon steaks in a shallow dish. Mix the oil, rosemary and seasoning together and brush over both sides of the steaks. Pour the remainder of the oil mixture on top of the steaks and marinate for at least thirty minutes.

Brush the barbecue grid with a little of the oil mixture. Place a few sprigs of fresh rosemary on the charcoal. Cook the salmon steaks over the fire for 10–20 minutes, turning and brushing with the marinade occasionally. Handle the salmon steaks very carefully while they are cooking to avoid them breaking up. Lift off with a fish slice and serve with lemon wedges.

## Vegetable Dishes

### Barbecued Corn on the Cob

Serves 4

4 fresh corn on the cob
(4oz) butter
1 tablespoon finely chopped fresh parsley
salt and freshly ground pepper

Fold back the husks from the corn and remove the silky hairs. Cut out the cob but retain the husk. Blanch the corn in boiling water for 7 minutes then drain and replace in the husks. Cook on the side of the fire for about 1 hour or until tender.

Mix the butter, parsley and seasoning together to serve with the hot corn.

Alternatively, remove the husks and place the corn in foil parcels with the parsley butter. Seal the parcels tightly enough to prevent the butter from seeping out as this will cause flames on the barbecue. Cook for 20-25 minutes or until the corn is tender.

### Courgette and Tomato Skewers

Serves 4

1lb courgettes cut into 2cm (¾in) thick slices
1 tablespoon lemon juice
salt and freshly ground pepper
8 small tomatoes
small onion, sliced into rings
1 tablespoon of oil

Blanch the courgette slices in boiling water for 1 minute. Drain well and sprinkle with lemon juice and pepper. Thread the tomatoes, courgettes and onion rings on to 4 skewers and brush with oil. Cook over the fire for 5–10 minutes, turning occasionally. Season with salt before serving.

CHAPTER 10

# Plant Lists

## BACKBONE PLANTING

Small trees and shrubs, grown in specially designed beds or in large containers, and a careful
selection of evergreen and perennial foliage
plants, will form the essential backbone of your
patio planting. This not only ensures year-round
interest, but also reduces the burden of
maintenance to the absolute minimum. Your
main framework of large plants will have to be
planned at the earliest stages, as this will influence
size and position of both paving and planting
spaces.

## Ornamental Trees and Shrubs

You should choose the smaller, compact or
dwarf species, varieties that will offer maximum
year-round interest. If your patio is well
sheltered, you may also be able to grow more
tender types. To keep trees and shrubs in peak
condition, regular watering, feeding and mulching
will be necessary. The heights below offer a
rough guide only.

**Abelia x grandiflora**   90cm (3ft). A small semi-
evergreen shrub with tiny pink or white flowers
in summer. The variety 'Gold Spot' has leaves
with an irregular central golden splash.

**Acer palmatum** (Japanese Maple)   2m (6ft). The
Japanese maples always offer excellent garden
value with their attractively shaped foliage,
especially for spring and autumn interest. Some
hybrids are more like small shrubs and are
perfect subjects for growing in containers. *A. p.*
Atropurpureum, for example, has purple-col-

oured foliage and the 'Dissectum' form is even
more delicate with feathery-cut foliage. *A. p.* 'D.
Crimson Queen' has a scarlet colouring whilst 'D.
Ornatum' turns from bronze to red in autumn.

**Berberis** (Barberry)   0.3–2.3m (12–90in). Both
evergreen and deciduous forms of this easily
grown and attractive prickly shrub have fine

*Fig II3   Shrubs and trees make equally good
subjects for containers: here a dwarf
rhododendron and scented honeysuckle grown
up a frame, soften the corner of a porch.*

Fig 114 Slow-growing evergreens, clipped into formal shapes, and dwarf conifers, can be grown in containers and added to your patio arrangement for height and perennial interest.

spring flowers and showy fruits. B. 'Nana' is slow growing and mound forming. *B. x antoniana* is an evergreen, also with a rounded habit, deep yellow flowers and blue-black berries. *B. aggregata* has red berries and good autumn colour.

**Buxus sempervirens** (Box) 30–40cm (12–16in). Classic slow-growing evergreen with tiny, glossy green leaves for clipping into hedge and topiary shapes. Balls, cones, pyramids and spirals look great in pots in a formal setting, whilst small hedges can be planted in troughs to create visual boundaries. Other forms are more ornamental: B. s. 'Elegantissima' makes a natural dome shape and has white markings and 'Gold Tip' has yellow tips.

**Arundinaria japonica** 4–5m (13–16ft). A hardy bamboo that thrives in half shade and which has glossy dark green ribbon-like leaves on the canes. It is a vigorous grower, so is perhaps better

restricted within a container. Compost must be kept moist.

**Arundinaria murieliae** (Elegant Bamboo) 2.4–3m (8–10ft). An attractive bamboo with bright green canes which turn yellow-green.

**Camellia japonica** 'Adolphe Audusson' 2.4m (8ft). A compact evergreen camellia with large blood-red blooms. It tolerates a fair amount of shade.

**Caryopteris** 1m (3ft). A small shrub valued for the soft effect of its grey leaves and blue flower spikes.

**Chamaecyparis lawsoniana** (Lawson) 2m (6ft). A popular cypress with drooping green foliage.

**Choisya ternata** (Mexican Orange Blossom) 3m (10ft). A cypress prized for its fragrant white flowers in late spring, early summer and its glossy

Fig 115   Choisya ternata *(Mexican Orange Blossom), showing attractive foliage.*

dark green leaves which are also aromatic when bruised. The smaller evergreen *C. t.* 'Sundance' has light yellow young foliage.

**Cordyline australis** (Cabbage Palm)   4.6m (15ft). Sword-like evergreen leaves and small creamy summer flowers.

**Corylus avellana** 'Contorta' (Cork-screw Hazel)   A small hazel grown for its ornamental spiral stems and showy catkins in late winter.

**Cotoneaster**   Choose from a large number of types most of which have ornamental berries, useful for late summer interest. *C. apiculatus* makes arching stems of small round leaves and red fruits, yet does not grow too large. *C. splendens* 'Sabrina' has small grey-green leaves and orange berries.

**Crataegus** (Thorn)   4.5m (15ft). The thorns are small ornamental trees with decorative fruits and fine spring blossom. *C. oxyacantha* 'Paul's Scarlet' has red double flowers.

**Daphne**   1.2m (4ft). Choose the smaller hybrids of this shrub, valued for its scented flowers in late winter/early spring. However, it is important to make sure the container is well drained. *D. laureola* is an evergreen with yellow-green flowers; *D. mezereum* thrives in shade and has purple-red flowers and red berries; *D. m.* 'Alba' has white flowers and amber fruits and 'Rosea' has rose-pink flowers. *D. odora* forms offer a similar range of colours and are shade-tolerant evergreens.

**Euonymus fortunei**   45cm (18in). There are various forms with attractive foliage for winter interest. Choose the smaller types like 'Emerald and Gold' which is bushy with gold markings, turning pink in winter, or 'Silver Queen' which has white markings.

**Fatsia japonica** (False Caster Oil Plant)   2m (6ft). A dramatic evergreen with glossy, palmate foliage which prefers part shade.

**Hydrangea macrophylla** (Lacecap Hydrangea)   1.5m (5ft). The large blooms come in various colours; 'Geoffrey Chadbuned' is red, 'Blaumeise' has blue flowers and 'White Wave' has white blooms.

**Ilex** (Holly)   1.2m (47in). There are many forms and colours, with or without spines. Variegated types are useful for different effects: the markings may be yellow, gold, white, cream or silver; stems could be purple, black or green and berries black, red, round or oval.

**Juniperus** (Juniper)   10–250cm (4–98in). There is a wide choice of varieties whose coloured, needle-like foliage is useful in winter. *J. chinensis* 'Pyramidalis' makes a slow-growing conical blue bush; spreading 'Gold Coast' is golden yellow; and 'Embley Park' has drooping branches of grass-green leaves.

**Lavandula** (Lavender)   45–100cm (18–40in). A highly aromatic and sun-loving small shrub which has various forms, all of which are evergreen: *L. angustifolia* 'Alba' has white flowers and narrow grey-green foliage; *L.a.* 'Rosea' has soft pink flowers and compact habit; 'Munstead' is larger but also compact with lavender-blue flowers.

*Fig 116   Lavandula with its delicately coloured bloom.*

**Laurus nobilis** (Sweet Bay)   1.5m (5ft). A classic evergreen shrub or standard-grown tree for sheltered areas. Its glossy green laurel-shaped leaves are aromatic and can be used in cooking. The foliage is often clipped into decorative shapes.

**Malus** (Flowering Crab)   3.6m (12ft). A small ornamental tree valued for its stunning spring blossom and interesting autumn fruits. There are many small varieties such as 'Golden Hornet' which has white flowers and plenty of yellow fruit; 'John Downie' whose large orange-red fruits are edible; and 'Red Jade' or 'Royal Beauty' which have red fruits and a weeping habit.

**Nandina domestica** (Heavenly Bamboo)   2.4m (8ft). A pretty bamboo with delicate pinnate leaves, white flowers and red berries.

**Nerium oleander**   4m (13½ft). A tender shrub with showy fragrant blooms.

**Phormium tenax**   2.4m (8ft). A good architectural foliage plant with large sword-like leaves. The hybrids offer colour options: bronze ('Bronze Baby'); black ('Dark Delight'); red ('Maori Chief'); apricot ('Apricot Queen'); even cream, purple and pink variations.

**Phyllostachys aurea** (Golden Bamboo)   2.4–3m (8–10ft). An evergreen bamboo with green canes that turn yellow.

**Prunus** (Flowering Cherry)   6m (20ft). Useful small trees producing excellent blossom and foliage colours. *P. rufa* 'Himalayan Cherry' has the added attraction of peeling red-brown or amber bark; *P. subhirtella* 'Autumnalis', the Autumn Cherry and its double or weeping hybrids, bloom at the end of summer.

**Pyrus** (Ornamental Pear)   4.5m (15ft). A group of small trees useful for special effects: for example, *P. salicifolia* 'Pendula'; the Weeping Silver Pear which has a weeping habit and silver foliage; and *P. communis* 'Beech Hill' which has good autumn colour.

**Robinia pseudoacacia** 'Frisia' (False Acacia)   5.4m (18ft). This is a small tree with eye-catching golden-yellow foliage which grows from spring to autumn.

**Rosmarinus** (Rosemary)   30–120cm (12–48in). A shrubby herb which enjoys full sun and looks good in tubs. The needle-like foliage is grey-green and the tiny flowers are blue.

**Salix** (Willow)   3m (10ft). The willow has a wide choice of shrub or tree forms, many with attractive foliage and interesting catkins, such as *S. helvetica* or *S. lanata*, the 'Woolly Willow', which is a downy slow grower.

**Sorbus** (Rowan)   5.4m (18ft). The Rowan has attractive foliage providing interest in spring, summer and autumn. Many have good berries too: 'Joseph Rock' (gold); 'Pearly King' (white/pink); *S. scalaris* (red berries).

**Taxus baccata** (Yew)   2.4m (8ft). A sombre dark green evergreen conifer which lends itself to being clipped into hedge and topiary shapes. It is a slow grower, so it could be grown in a container.

**Trachycarpus fortunei** (Hardy Palm) 2–3m (6–10ft). A good architectural foliage plant with dramatic fan-shaped leaves.

**Viburnum davidii** 75cm (30in). This is the smallest of the Viburnums with glossy leaves and light blue berries.

**Yucca** 1–2m (3–6ft). A dramatic foliage plant with sword-shaped leaves and creamy-white flower spikes.

## Dwarf Rhododendrons and Azaleas

Dwarf forms of these superb flowering shrubs are perfect for growing in tubs and containers. Tubs and containers will enable you to maintain an acid soil, which is an advantage as rhododendrons and azaleas are lime haters and do not always do well in the garden. Do not let the compost dry out and combine them with heathers and dwarf conifers who enjoy the same conditions.

**Japanese Azaleas** 50–75cm (20–30in). These are mostly evergreen or semi-evergreen but are prone to late frost, so protect them from early morning sun. The range of colours includes 'Blue Danube' with striking blue blooms; 'Hinomayo' which makes a mass of pink flowers in late spring; or 'Johanna' which has bright red flowers against shiny dark green foliage.

**Deciduous Azaleas** 1.2–1.5m (4–5ft). These are hardy with wonderful flowers and good autumn colour – allow them full sun or light shade. 'Persil' has white trumpets with an orange-yellow flare and 'Klondyke' has scented orange flowers and copper-coloured young foliage.

**Dwarf Rhododendrons** 15–90cm (6–35in). You will have a wide choice of sizes, colours and forms including the compact and free-flowering *yakushimanum* hybrids, which include bright red against green, 'Dopey', and the low-growing 'Grumpy' which has pink-tinged yellow trumpets. Another rhododendron worth considering, is tiny 'Chikor', which has a mass of yellow flowers in late spring at a height of 15–20cm (6–8in). The unusual 'Ramapo' 30–40cm (12–16in) which has glaucous green foliage and pale violet flowers is also very attractive.

## Conifers

Dwarf and slow-growing conifers are perfect for containers and patio beds, as they are compact in size and offer an interesting range of shapes and colours. This means that they can be an important element of your backbone planting scheme. Many species will naturally grow into domes, pyramids and spires in a choice of blue, green, gold and silver foliage colours.

Fig 117 Japanese Azaleas showing a mass of pink blooms.

**Abies concolor** 'Compacta' 60–90cm (24–35in). A dwarf fir with an irregular rounded habit and bright silver-blue leaves.

**A. koreana** 1.5–2m (5–6½ft). The dark green upper leaves are silvery-white beneath, with eye-catching blue cylindrical cones.

**A. nordmanniana** 'Golden Spreader' 20–30cm (8–12in). A neat bush of golden yellow needles.

**Cedrus libani** 'Sargentii' 60–90cm (24–35in). This plant's weeping habit produces a dense spread of green.

**Chamaecyparis lawsoniana** (Aurea Densa) 30–50cm (12–20in). It makes a dense dome of golden-yellow foliage.

**C.l.** 'Ellwood's Pillar' 75–100cm (30–39in). It produces a narrow compact pillar of feathery blue-grey.

**C.l.** 'Gnome' 20–30cm (8–12in). A tiny deep green specimen.

**C.l.** 'Little Spire' 1.5–2m (5–6.5ft). It grows slowly into a green column which eventually produces attractive red 'flowers' in spring.

**C.l.** 'Nana Albospica' 25cm (30in). The white foliage looks almost like snow in summer.

**C.l.** 'Pygmy' 30cm (12in). It makes a tiny mound of grey-green leaves.

**C. Pisifera** 'Gold Spangle' 90cm (35in). 'Gold Spangle' has a rounded habit and bright gold foliage for good winter colour.

**C.p.** 'Plumosa Compressa' 20–30cm (8–12in). A tiny, compact mound of pale yellow foliage.

**C.p.** 'Plumosa Purple Dome' 50–60cm (20–24in). The feathery grey foliage has a purple tint in winter.

**C. thyoides** 'Rubicon' 60cm (24in). Its compact bronze-green foliage turns a rich red in winter.

**Cryptomeria japonica** 'Compressa' 30–40cm (12–16in). A small and compact tree forming a flat-topped globe of green foliage, which is tinted a reddish-purple in winter.

**C.j.** 'Vilmoriniana' 30–40cm (12–16in). It grows slowly to produce a neat globe of fresh green.

**Microbiota decussata** 20–30cm (8–12in). This has a low-growing spread of lacy but dense green foliage which turns bronze in winter.

**Picea abies** 'Little Gem' 20–30cm (8–12in). It makes a dense ball of green, with attractive new shoots in spring.

**P. glauca** 'Aurina' 40cm (16in). This fresh green, compact pyramid is the ideal miniature for sink and container gardens.

**P. mariana** 'Nana' 15–20cm (6–8in). A slow-growing blue ball, perfect for troughs and sinks.

**Pinus mugo** 'Humpy' 30–40cm (12–16in). It makes a dense round bush of short green needles and has prominent winter buds.

*Fig 118  An example of a young* Pinus mugo.

?.m. 'Wintergold' 40–50cm (16–20in). This tree has a bright golden form throughout winter, turning to light green during summer.

?. **pumila** 'Dwarf Blue' 40–50cm (16–20in). A slow-growing spreader, producing clusters of blue and white needles.

?. **strobus** 'Reinshaus' 60cm (24in). A small compact bush that needs good drainage. It makes a dense display of glaucous needles.

?. **sylvestris** 'Hibernica' 50–60cm (20–24in). It makes a compact round bush of grey-blue needles and prominent winter buds.

**Taxus baccata** (Corley's Coppertip') 30–40cm (12–16in). Its copper-coloured leaves turn to green with whitish markings. It is a semi-prostrate form.

**T.b.** 'Summergold' 40–50cm (16–20in). This has bright golden-yellow foliage in summer.

**Thuja occidentalis** 'Danica' 30–45cm (12–18in). A compact globe of dark green that turns bronze in winter.

**T. orientalis** 'Golden Ball' 40–50cm (16–20in). A dome-shaped bush of bright yellow that turns green and later bronze.

**T. plicata** 'Rogersii' 30–45cm (12–18in). It is good for winter colour turning from green to golden bronze.

**Tsuga canadensis** 'Jeddeloh' 30–40cm (12–16in). A graceful light green foliage and a semi-prostrate habit.

# Climbers

Climbing plants are essential in the well-planned patio; they are needed for covering and disguising walls and fences or to provide valuable vertical interest on trellises, screens and special supports.

**Actinidia chinensis** (Chinese Gooseberry) This has creamy-white flowers and large heart-shaped leaves. It likes plenty of sun. Both male and female plants produce the familiar hairy, egg-shaped, edible fruits.

**Clematis** There are a large number of types, both evergreen and deciduous, and they are grown for their spectacular range of flowers. Choose your own favourites from large or small blooms, scented types, shade or sun lovers.

**Clerodendrum thomsoniae** A climber producing a mass of red and white flowers.

**Jasminum nudiflorum** (Winter Jasmine) This has delicate green foliage with flowers appearing on the naked branches during the winter.

**Lonicera** (Honeysuckle) There are various forms of this popular country climber including evergreen and deciduous types, and also those with night- or day-scented flowers.

**Parthenocissus quinquefolia** (Virginia Creeper) This climber gives good foliage cover, and the leaves turn a brilliant orange and scarlet in autumn.

**Vitis vinifera** (Grape Vine) A useful foliage climber. 'Purpurea' has claret to deep purple foliage.

# Ivies

Ivies make excellent evergreen cover for walls, trellises and fences — anywhere where you require a quick cover-up or the vertical interest of a living curtain all year round. They can also be used as ground-cover plants, encouraged to trail down from hanging baskets or disguise the edge of tubs. There is a spectacular range of different shapes and colours among the Hedera genus, such as silvers and bronzes, dark and light greens, gold, white, cream and even pink markings.

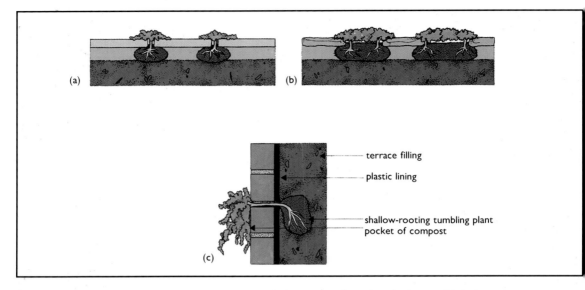

Fig 119  *Interplanting low-growing creepers in the cracks between walls and paving is a useful device for softening hard surfaces and adding colour and interest to your scheme: (a) scrape out the sand between paving joints and replace it with potting compost for creeping plants; (b) leaving spaces or gaps between paving is also a useful way to add plants to your patio scheme; (c) leave spaces in walls and fill them with compost for inserting shallow-rooted trailing plants.*

**Hedera canariensis** (Canary Island Ivy)  The large leaves turn bronze in winter. Silvery-grey and cream-white variegated forms are also available.

**H. colchica** 'Dentata' (Persian Ivy)  It has particularly large leaves; the variety 'Sulphur Heart' has yellow splashes; and 'Variegata' has creamy yellow margins.

**H. helix** (Common Ivy)  A useful ivy that will grow almost anywhere, even in very shady conditions. There are many variations.

**H.h.** 'Cavendishii'  This has small mottled grey leaves with cream margins.

**H.h.** 'Chicago'  The small leaves are blotched with bronze-purple.

**H.h.** 'Deltoidea'  The heart-shaped leaves make dense cover that turns bronze in winter.

**H.h.** 'Glacier'  It has silver-grey leaves with white margins.

**H.h.** 'Goldheart'  There is a central yellow splash to each leaf.

**H.h.** 'Manda's Crested'  A slow grower with a reddish colour in winter.

**H.h.** 'Marginata Elegantissima'  It has small grey-green leaves that have pink edges in winter.

**H.h.** 'Sagittifolia'  It has interesting five-lobed shaped leaves. There is a cream variegated form.

## Hardy Ferns

Ferns with their strong feathery fronds make useful foliage contrasts to glossier, larger-leaved plants. A single specimen can look stunning in its own pot or container, as can a collection of different varieties planned for a large bed in a shady

Fig 120   *The Maidenhair fern (*Adiantum pedatum*).*

position. Keep the beds and containers filled with moist compost and mulch any areas of bare soil with small pebbles or bark chips.

**Adiantum pedatum** (Maidenhair Fern) 25cm (10in). A very hardy fern with dainty foliage.

**Asplenium trichomanes** (Spleenwort) 7.5–15cm (3–6in). This fern produces thread-like black stalks with green lobes.

**Athyrium filix femina** (Lady Fern) 30cm (24in). It makes tufts of light green fronds.

**Blechnum penna marina** 7.5–10cm (3–4in). The young fronds have a coppery colour. This low-growing fern makes an attractive carpet of small flattened fronds with more erect short fertile fronds.

**Blechnum spicant** (Hard Fern) 25–30cm (10–12in). A useful fern in that it tolerates dry conditions.

**Dryopteris dilatata** (Broad Buckler Fern) 60–100cm (24–39in). This has broad, divided fronds.

113

**Dryopteris filix-mas** (Male Fern) 60–100cm (24–39in). A reliable fern, frequently seen in the wild. It produces a large clump of tough green fronds.

**Matteuccia struthiopteris** (Ostrich Feather Fern) 1–1.5m (3–5ft). An attractive ornamental fern with large feathery fronds.

**Onoclea sensibilis** (Sensitive Fern) 50cm (20in). A pretty fern that prefers moist conditions.

**Osmunda regalis** (Royal Fern) 1.2–2m (4–6.5ft). A large dramatic clump of fronds.

**Phyllitis scolopendrium** (Hart's Tongue Fern) 50cm (20in). A good contrast, with flat tongue-like fronds covered in brown spores. An evergreen that is useful for winter interest.

**Polypodium vulgare** (Common Polypody) 25–30cm (10–12in). A good evergreen that tolerates chalk.

*Fig 121  An attractively shaped Hosta (H. sieboldiana 'Elegans').*

**Polystichum aculeatum** (Hard Shield Fern) 50–60cm (20–24in). An evergreen with strong, dark green fronds.

**Polystichum lonchitis** (Holly Fern) 30–100cm (12–39in). It makes dense tufts of evergreen fronds.

**Polystichum setiferum** 'Plumoso-divisilobum' (Soft Shield Fern) 50cm (20in). This has finely divided feathery fronds.

## Hostas

Hostas or plantain lilies, offer an excellent range of plant shapes and colours with their large pleated foliage, and are the perfect contrast to feathery or delicate leaves. They include an interesting range of leaf colours and patterns.

*Fig 122 An old stone sink is perfect for displaying a collection of alpine plants.*

**Hosta albo-marginata** 15–20cm (6–8in). This has light green leaves with cream margins. Its striped flowers are mauve and white.

**H.** 'Elegans' 60cm (24in). It has large, round silver-grey leaves with deep indentations.

**H. fortunei** 'Albopicta' 40–50cm (16–20in). This plant has oval yellow-edged leaves which develop dark green margins with age. There is a completely yellow form in spring and summer called 'Aurea'.

**H.** 'Frances Williams' 50–60cm (20–24in). It displays spectacular blue-grey leaves with beige markings.

**H.** 'Halcyon' 30cm (12in). **H.** 'Halcyon' has heart-shaped blue leaves and lilac flowers.

**H.** 'Honeybells' 30cm (12in). The mauve flowers are scented. The leaves are green.

**H. lancifolia** 15–18cm (6–7in). It has narrow shiny green leaves.

**H.** 'Thomas Hogg' 30cm (12in). The deep green leaves have a wide cream margin. Summer flowers are lilac.

**H. undulata** 50cm (20in). The wavy green leaves have a central white band.

## Alpines

If you are planning an informal or small stone sink rock-garden, you will find a fascinating variety of delicate alpine plant forms to make up your special collection. The majority of these fragile species are low-growing, creating spreading cushions or carpets of colour.

There is a vast range of unusual and stunning flowering plants suitable for free-draining, rocky conditions. This is a small selection of what will be available in the specialist section of your local garden centre.

*Fig 123   A Campanula in full bloom.*

**Alyssum**   This cushion-forming alpine has a mass of tiny flowers that can be white, yellow or pink.

**Armeria**   This makes a green mat below a mass of pink pompon heads.

**Aubrieta**   This is a popular mat-forming alpine which displays dense growth of mauve, purple or red flowers.

**Campanula** (Bellflower)   This has tussocks of pretty blue to mauve bell- or star-shaped flowers.

**Chrysanthemum hosmariense** (Alpine Chrysanthemum)   This alpine plant has silver leaves and daisy-like flowers, which appear from spring to autumn.

**Cyananthus** (Trailing Bellflower)   A mat-forming trailer with coloured foliage and blue flowers.

**Cypripedium**   A stunning group of orchids, some of which are very hardy.

**Dianthus** (Rock Pinks)   10–45cm (4–18in). A wide range of sweet-scented pink to almost red flowers with stripes and other markings. **Dianthus** also have white or silver foliage.

**Edelweiss**   This very popular plant has woolly foliage and small white felt-like flowers.

**Gentiana** (Gentian)   It has slender narrow leaves and beautiful blue trumpet flowers.

**Helianthemum** (Rock Rose)   It is like a tiny wild rose.

**Potentilla** (Cinquefoil)   A colourful summer plant with frondy foliage and rose-like blooms.

**Primula**   A familiar favourite for spring with their clump of thick-veined leaves and beautifully deep-coloured flowers.

**Ramonda**   A rosette-forming plant with rough hairy leaves and mauve-blue flowers.

**Saxifrage**   A large group of plants with interesting clump-forming foliage and pretty flower clusters.

**Sedum** (Stonecrop)   A wide range of sprawling plants with small fleshy evergreen leaves and heads of pink or yellow flowers.

## Heaths and Heathers

Heaths and heathers, producing clumps and carpets of dense colour, are useful for creating permanent effects according to season. Experiment with winter- and autumn-flowering types to maintain interest throughout the year.

**Calluna vulgaris**   10–60cm (4–24in). There are many interesting hybrid forms of the evergreen common heather or ling. These are just a few of the colour variations:

**C.v.** 'Alba Plena'   50cm (20in). It has double white flowers in summer.

**C.v.** 'Beoley Gold'   45cm (18in). A late summer plant with white flowers and golden leaves.

**C.v.** 'Blazeaway'   50cm (20in). It has mauve flowers in late summer, and the leaves turn red in winter.

**C.v.** 'Gold Haze' 50cm (20in). It has white flowers and gold foliage.

**C.v.** 'Orange Queen' 60cm (24in). This has pink flowers and gold foliage which turns orange.

**C.v.** 'Robert Chapman' 30–60cm (12–24in). This plant displays mauve flowers and golden leaves which turn orange and then red.

**C.v.** 'Silver Queen' 60cm (24in). A plant with silver-grey leaves and pale mauve flowers.

**C.v.** 'Sister Anne' 10cm (4in). It has grey foliage with pink flowers.

**C.v.** 'Tib' 30–60cm (12–24in). 'Tib' has double rosy-red flowers.

**Erica arborea** (Tree Heath) 25cm (10in). The fragrant white flowers appear in early spring. Hybrids produce purple flowers.

**E. carnea** 25cm (10in). A winter-flowering, lime-tolerant heather, offering a wide choice of colours such as: 'Adrienne Duncan' with red flowers and dark bronze-green foliage; 'Foxhollow' which has pale pink flowers and yellow foliage with a red tinge in winter; 'Pink Spangles' makes a mass of pink flowers in winter; and 'Springwood White' has white winter blooms.

**E. cinerea** (Bell Heather) 15–25cm (6–10in). This summer flowering plant comes in a wide choice of colours: 'Domino' is white; 'Golden Drop' has pink flowers but golden foliage which turns rusty-red in winter; and 'P. S. Patrick' has purple flowers.

**E. mediterranea** 2m (6ft). A very small plant with rose-red spring flowers. It is lime tolerant. The hybrids include grey and green foliage and white flowers.

**E. vagans** (Cornish Heath) 1.2m (4ft). This plant makes long sprays of flowers from summer

*Fig 124   An example of* Calluna vulgaris.

through to autumn. There are many varieties with pink, white and cerise flowers and yellow foliage.

**E.x. williamsii** 'D. Williams' 10–25cm (4–18in). It has rose-pink flowers in the summer through to the autumn. The yellow-tipped leaves turn bronze by winter.

# COLOUR AND INTEREST THROUGH THE YEAR

When carefully planned, a blend of annuals, bulbs and perennials can put on a beautiful patio display which can be enjoyed right through the seasons.

## Spring Interest

**Clivia miniata** (Kaffir Lily) 50cm (1½ft). This plant is very elegant with bold, tongue-like leaves and large clusters of orange, trumpet-shaped blooms.

**Cheiranthus cheiri** (Wallflowers) 38–46cm (15–18in). This is useful for rich early colours – plant it into tubs when bushy before winter. Look out for the new compact forms in pastel colours.

**Chionodoxa** (Glory of the Snow) 7.5–10cm (3–4in). It is grown for its pretty blue star-shaped flowers.

**Crocus** 5–13cm (2–5in). Plant these in massed groups to get the best effect from their low carpet of bright, waxy colour. They are good for planting under taller spring flowers and offer a choice of large or small, open or closed blooms, and a range of colours from purples, golds, pinks and whites to striped patterns.

*Fig 125  A lovely mixed display for late spring.*

**Cyclamineus narcissi** 20–30cm (8–12in). There are various colour types and a dwarf habit that makes them excellent for tubs.

**Erythroniums** 30cm (12in). There are various types with their lovely spotted foliage and beautiful nodding blooms. They are very useful, since they will tolerate light shade. 'The Trout Lily', *E. californicum* has cream flowers; and *E. denscanis*, 'Dog's Tooth Violet', has mauve to pink flowers.

**Freesia refracta** 50cm (1½ft). These are sweet-scented, delicate flowers in a blend of clear, complementary colours.

**Galanthus** (Snowdrop) 10–25cm (4–10in). These tiny heralds of spring are usually the first to be seen, pushing their white bells through snow or chilly soil as early as the New Year. Look out for varieties with larger flowers, frills or interesting green markings.

**Garden Hyacinths** 30–38cm (12–15in). The best hyacinths for tubs and containers are the Multiflora types which produce several spikes of white, blue or pink: 'Pink Pearl' and 'Anna Marie' are pink; 'Carnegie' is white; 'City of Harlem' is yellow; and the early 'Ostara' and 'Delft Blue' have blue spikes.

**Muscari** (Grape Hyacinth) 15–20cm (6–8in). The tiny grape hyacinth with its miniature spikes of deep, dark blue and delicate scent can look superb beneath other taller plants or fronting a window-box display.

**Narcissi and Daffodils** 38–61cm (12–24in). There are a wide range of colours and styles, including double flowers, frills and special markings, if you want to create a display of particular interest: *N.* 'Salome' which has a pink crown; *N.* 'Marie Jose', a butterfly type with yellow star-shaped markings; and *N.* 'Petit Four' which is a double-flowered type with peach-coloured frilly centres.

**Narcissus asturiensis** 8–10cm (3–4in). A miniature early-flowering form with a wide range of flower types including tiny trumpet daffodils.

**Narcissi jonquilla** 15–25cm (6–10in). A sweet-scented variety that does well in tubs.

**Narcissi triandrus** 15–40cm (6–16in). A shorter-growing, multi-headed variety with interesting bloom shapes.

**Polyanthus** 18cm (7in). These are popular for their dense display of bright flowers amongst thick green leaves. There are many colour variations.

**Primula** 18cm (7in). The semi-miniature, early-flowering Primroses are prettiest for pots.

**Scilla** (Woodland Bluebells) 10cm (4in). These have delicate nodding bells of blue, white and pink.

**Tulips** 30–66cm (12–26in). These are valuable for adding exactly the colour you want later in the season. Tulips are available in an extra-ordinary range of shades and shapes from single and double early blooms to special hybrids and late-blooming types, exotic Parrot tulips, elegant lily-flowered varieties, blacks, reds, whites, blues, yellows – even stripes and frills.

**Tulipa Greigii** 15–30cm (6–12in). A dwarf type good for window-boxes and tubs and available in a range of colours: 'Princess Charmante' is scented; and 'Red Riding Hood' is red with stripes.

## Summer Interest

**Alyssum** 8–10cm (3–4in). It makes a close-growing carpet of white or gold, which is useful for edging or softening the rim of containers. The white is handy for positioning with stronger deeper colours that need lightening.

**Antirrhinum** 20–30cm (8–12in). It is easy to grow in a wide range of colours – dwarf forms like 'Little Gem' are best for pots.

**African Marigold** 25–60cm (10in–2ft). The large golden blooms are a real eye-catcher and plants come in a choice of sizes from tall, standing at 60cm (2ft), middling at 46–60cm (18–24in) and low-growing at 25–30cm (10–14in).

**Begonia semperflorens** 25–50cm (9–18in). These are valued for their combination of glossy green leaves and waxy flowers in shades of red, pink and white.

**Calceolaria** 25cm (10in). It makes a mass of golden bubbles against green foliage.

**Campanula fragilis** (Basket Campanula) This creeper has trailing stems of large, pale blue flowers which can look superb in pots and hanging baskets. Other forms have purple or dark blue flowers.

**Cineraria maritima** 23–30cm (9–12in). It is prized for its crisped silver foliage, and is a good highlight and companion to other plants. It likes a sunny situation.

**Coleus blumei** 50cm (1.5ft). These are strongly marked, coloured foliage plants in shades of dark red, yellow, green, cream and black.

**Dianthus** 10–45cm (4–18in). The pretty pinks and carnations make a sweet-scented addition to old-fashioned tubs and pots in shades of pink, white and red.

**French Marigolds** 30cm (12in). A splendid range of free-flowering golden blooms against feathery green foliage.

**Fuchsia** 60cm (2ft). The many hybrid forms produce both large and small exotic dangling blooms in purple, pink and white. They are ex-cellent in hanging baskets and tubs.

Fig 126   Use raised beds for colourful summer bedding, as they are easy
to plant and maintain and are excellent for disabled patio gardeners.

Fig 127   French marigolds will add a lovely splash of colour to containers
all summer.

*Fig 128 Petunias provide a colourful massed display in summer.*

**Geranium** 30–38cm (12–15in). These are always popular plants for pots with their attractive foliage and red, pink and white flowers. Choose varieties specially recommended for growing in pots and tubs: the ivy-leaved types are good for hanging baskets; and the cascading and trailing types are useful for balconies and hanging baskets over which they can trail 46cm (18in). Some have scented leaves, and can be positioned close at hand on a patio or in a scented garden.

**Impatiens** (Busy Lizzie) 25cm (10in). It will tolerate cool shade, producing the familiar profusion of red, pink, white or striped flowers.

**Lobelia** 30cm (12in). The cascade types are perfect for hanging baskets making a ball of pink or purple flowers. They combine well with other plants, or you can grow several shades in the one container.

**Lysimachia nummularia** (Creeping Jenny) This creeper's tiny green leaves and yellow flowers are useful for window-boxes and hanging baskets providing the soil is kept moist.

**Mimulus** (Monkey Flower) 15–30cm (6–12in). The Monkey Flower provides good strong colour for window-boxes and hanging baskets, the flowers come in strong burgundy and gold, and some of them are interestingly blotched.

**Paludosum** (Miniature Marguerite) 23–30cm (9–12in). The feathery green foliage is studded with daisies.

**Pansies** 15–20cm (6–8in). There are a great many different velvet colours and markings for creating special combinations.

**Petunia** 30cm (12in). These compact forms are good for hanging baskets and produce a mass of frilled and sometimes striped trumpets of purple, pink, blue, red or yellow.

**Pot Marigolds** 30–38cm (12–15in). These give a reliable display of golden flowers and green foliage.

**Salvia** 25–30cm (10–12in). Long lasting and popular for its bright red spikes above marked green fleshy foliage.

**Sedum sieboldii variegatum** A pretty cream creeper and blue or green foliage.

**Tagetes** 23cm (9in). Many varieties forming mounds of tiny yellow, gold or bronze flowers among the dense, bright green feathery foliage.

**Tropaeolum majus** (Nasturtium) 23cm (9in). Attractive bright green leaves and gaily coloured yellow and orange flowers that flourish in poor soil and hot dry conditions. 23cm/9in indicates the shorter forms.

**Verbena** 15–30cm (6–12in). Pointed leaves and flowers ranging from purple to scarlet or blue.

## Roses

Roses are an attractive permanent feature within a romantic or old-fashioned patio scheme, and the smaller forms of the compact bush roses can do well in containers or raised beds. Keep them watered and mulched well, feeding generously during the flowering season. There are various basic types to choose from:

**Roses** (Hybrid Tea)  Types reach 75cm (30in). 'Abbeyfield' Rose is large-flowered and low-growing with a compact habit, and is a soft red; 'Pot o' Gold' is small and bushy, and has scented yellow/gold flowers.

**Cluster Flowered Bush Roses** (Floribundas)  Smaller types grow to 45cm (18in). This rose displays a variety of excellent colours and has plenty of compact forms – often called Patio Roses: 'Elegant Pearl' is dense, compact and long flowering with creamy white flowers; 'Gentle Touch' produces pink flowers in clusters: and 'Robin Redbreast' is dark red with a yellow or white eye.

**Ramblers and Climbers**  1.8m (6ft). These grow over a frame or nearby trellis: 'Swany' has double white blooms and thrives in shade; 'Bobbie James' produces small, fragrant cream flowers; and 'Paul's Scarlet Climber' is a semi-double brilliant red form.

**Miniature Roses**  30cm (12in). These are pretty for small containers with delicate foliage and tiny pink, white or red flowers.

*Fig 129   The ever popular rose can be used for summer colour.*

# Autumn Interest

**Begonia tuberhybrida** (Tuberous Begonia) 30cm (12in). These are grand and colourful with their bright blooms. The Pendula types are best for hanging baskets, and you could choose 'Multiflora Maxima' for tubs.

**Bergenia** (Elephants Ears) 30cm (12in). This is mainly grown for its giant fleshy leaves but produces extremely pretty white, pink or red flowers.

**Dwarf Chrysanthemums** 30–38cm (12–15in). These are pompon types in rich autumn shades of red and gold.

**Colchicum autumnale** 10–15cm (4–6in). There are various free-flowering varieties, producing mauve or white star-shaped flowers.

**Crinum x powellii** 60–90cm (2–3ft). A tender plant for sheltered spots with Amaryllis-like, huge, scented trumpets of pink or white.

**Cyclamen** 8cm (3in). There are various winter- and autumn-flowering types. The cluster of butterfly-like blooms are white or pink, making an exotic splash of shape and colour. Some are scented.

**Galtonia candicans** 60–76cm (2–2.5ft). It produces spikes of white bell-like flowers.

**Iris danfordiae** 5cm (2in). This plant has yellow flowers.

**Iris histrioides** 5cm (2in). It has blue blooms in late autumn/winter.

**Nerine bowdenii** 45cm (18in). It has lovely pink lily-like flowers.

**Ranunculus** 30cm (12in). There is a wide variety of pinks, yellows and reds, with a choice of double or semi-double forms.

**Solanum capsicastrum** (Winter Cherry) 23–38cm (9–15in). A good splash of colour for window-boxes and small pots. The plants are like miniature green bushes studded with bright orange 'Cherries'.

**Sternbergia lutea** 15cm (6in). It has flowers like a yellow crocus.

**Vallota speciosa** (Scarborough Lily) 60cm (2ft). A tender but spectacular plant for sheltered areas, with its brilliant red trumpet flowers.

**Zephyranthes candida** 15–30cm (6–12in). A tender plant with white starry flowers and grass-like leaves.

# Edibles

Many fruits and vegetables adapt well to being container grown, particularly compact and tender varieties which can be supplied with tubs of the correct compost and positioned to catch exactly the right amount of sun or shade. For those with only small gardens, a patio vegetable patch may be the only way to taste the delights of your own produce. Plants will require conscientious watering and feeding during the growing season.

**Aubergine** 90cm (3ft). 'Slim Jim' is a decorative plant with purple leaves and small fruits 7cm (3in) long.

**Corn Salad** 10cm (4in). Sometimes called 'Lambs Lettuce', this is a tasty salad plant that can be grown almost all year round. The narrow leaves are eaten young.

**Mini Cucumbers** These can be grown indoors or on a sheltered patio in 25cm (10in) pots. 'Petita F' produces cucumbers 20cm (8in) long.

**Dwarf French Bean** 30cm (12in). 'Royal Burgundy' has attractive purple flowers and purple pods, so it is decorative as well as useful.

Fig 130  Plastic growing bags enable a wide range of tender vegetables to be grown on the patio.

Fig 131  Tomatoes can be ripened in the sun on the patio.

**Lettuce**  Grow the more decorative varieties like 'Novita' which makes an ornamental ball of curved leaves.

**Peas**  45cm (18in). A dwarf, early variety like 'Hurst Beagle' which has a good flavour, could be grown in a container.

**Sweet Pepper**  30–40cm (12–16in). Plants with a dwarf habit like *Capsicum* 'Redskin F' are ideal for tubs and produce fruits around a central stem.

**Radish**  45cm (18in). A tasty treat from the minimum of space, 'Cherry Bell' is a fast grower making round, red radishes, and 'China Rose' is a winter radish, which is long and pink.

**Tomatoes**  45cm (18in). Some varieties are perfect for pots or even strawberry containers. Choose a self-supporting type with fruits lustered round a central stem for growing in ubs, or one of the tiny cherry tomato types like weet-tasting 'Small Fry'.

## Herbs

Herbs are very well suited to pots of all sizes, whether it be a tiny pot on a shelf or table, or a large tub to stand on the patio. You can put together a collection of your own favourites to use in cooking or simply grow them for the decorative effect of the scented flowers and foliage.

**Bush Basil**   25cm (10in). *Ocimum minimum* with small compact foliage is the best for pots.

Fig 132   A formal patio that is both ornamental and useful, displaying a wide range of herbs and vegetables.

*Fig 133   An example of a strong scented curry plant showing yellow summer flowers.*

**Chives**   23cm (9in). Their spiky grass-like foliage and pink pompon flowers are a good contrast to other plants.

**Garlic Chives**   30cm (12in). These are chives with a mild garlic-onion flavour and white flowers.

**Marjoram**   25–30cm (10–12in). This is an attractive bush of small leaves and soft pink flowers.

**Mint**   15cm (6in). There are many varieties with different scents and flavours and including variegated foliage types. Container growing helps to limit vigorous growth which normally makes mints unsuitable in the garden.

**Parsley**   15–30cm (6–12in). 'Curlina' is a tightly curled compact form, which is dark green and very attractive – it is ideal for pots.

**Rosemary**   0.6–1.2m (2–4ft). An excellent shrubby bush of spiky foliage and soft blue flowers.

**Sage**   30cm (12in). A soft grey or purple foliage plant, although it does produce attractive flowers in summer.

**Savory**   30–45cm (1–1½ft). Summer and winter varieties make an attractive small-leaved plant, and it is a useful pot herb.

**Tarragon**   1m (3ft). The French type has the better flavour. The narrow flat green leaves make it an attractive plant.

**Thyme**   23–30cm (9–12in). Many varieties offer variegated and coloured foliage forms, including creeping thymes which make excellent plants for softening the edges of pots.

# Index